Studying for

SOCIAL
WORK

Dr Eileen Baldry is Professor, Social Work program, School of Social Sciences and International Studies, University of South Wales. She recently served as Associate Dean (Education) in the Faculty of Arts and Social Sciences. She teaches social policy, community development and criminology and researches in social justice, prisons, Indigenous social work, mental and cognitive disability.

Dr Mark Hughes is an Associate Professor in Social Welfare at Southern Cross University. Mark has worked as a social worker in health, mental health and aged care settings in the UK and Australia. He is co-author of five books and a range of publications on social work practice, organisational practice, working with older people, and gay and lesbian ageing.

Linda Burnett is a Learning Adviser at the Learning Centre, University of New South Wales. She teaches academic writing and communication, with a focus on integrating writing skills development within specific disciplinary frameworks. She is particularly interested in questions of identity and voice in writing.

Dr Ian Collinson is an associate lecturer in the Dept. of Media, Music, Communication and Cultural Studies at Macquaire University. He has been teaching academic writing and literacy skills for over a decade, with a special interest in learning to write within specific disciplinary contexts.

Studying for
SOCIAL
WORK

EILEEN BALDRY, MARK HUGHES,
LINDA BURNETT AND IAN COLLINSON

SAGE

Los Angeles | London | New Delhi
Singapore | Washington DC

SAGE Publications Ltd
1 Oliver's Yard
55 City Road
London EC1Y 1SP

SAGE Publications Inc.
2455 Teller Road
Thousand Oaks, California 91320

SAGE Publications India Pvt Ltd
B 1/I 1 Mohan Cooperative Industrial Area
Mathura Road
New Delhi 110 044

SAGE Publications Asia-Pacific Pte Ltd
33 Pekin Street #02-01
Far East Square
Singapore 048763

Library of Congress Control Number: 2010941593

British Library Cataloguing in Publication data

A catalogue record for this book is available from the British Library

ISBN 978-1-84860-124-6
ISBN 978-1-84860-125-3 (pbk)

Typeset by C&M Digitals (P) Ltd, Chennai, India
Printed at CPI Antony Rowe, Chippenham, Wiltshire
Printed on paper from sustainable resources

CONTENTS

INTRODUCTION

In this chapter we introduce the book and set the context for studying social work. In particular we examine:

- issues related to learning about social work in a university environment;
- challenges for new social work students, such as balancing time commitments and becoming used to information and communication technology;
- different approaches to using or developing knowledge in practice, including the relevance of two threshold concepts: evidence-based practice and critical reflective practice.

I need to be open and I need to be honest or I'm not going to learn. And if I don't put it out there, then how am I going to learn? … I didn't come here to get a piece of paper. I came to be an effective worker and I think that's the bottom line for me. (SW student)

Such a genuine and committed approach to learning for social work is supported and enhanced by effective study skills. However, as with professional practice skills, the skills needed to survive and flourish at university do not necessarily come automatically. They need to be identified, practised and refined so that you can gain the most you possibly can from the learning opportunities offered and, also, get that piece of paper at the end. In fact, as one student observed in a most insightful comment: 'It's very helpful to think of yourself not as a student, but as a social worker in the making'. So this book is not just a study skills guide; it supports your development as a social worker.

The book is designed to assist you in developing your academic capacity and confidence so that you can meet the requirements of your social work degree. In particular, it aims to help improve your written and spoken communication in academic contexts, as well as highlighting the relevance of these for social work practice. You can learn better, develop more effective reading and analytical skills, access information easier, and make better use of your time in undertaking academic work. We have used quotes from interviews we conducted with social work students in Australia and from other publications, acknowledging of course the source of these other student quotes. In this way we have attempted to ground the book in the experiences, needs, and contexts of students studying for social work. The book aims to reduce concerns and anxieties about academic work and is relevant to both younger students and those returning to study after lengthy periods in the workforce.

UNIVERSITIES AND PROFESSIONAL SOCIAL WORK

I question why I'm here sometimes and you have to. I am aware that I [will be] working with people's lives and the role that I play could be extremely critical, usually is extremely critical for most people. And I don't take that lightly. I don't take that lightly at all. And I am learning a lot and I love learning. … Being my age and coming to uni and actually achieving – 'Whoa!'. I think that's pretty cool. Yeah, so that's a good feeling. (SW student)

One of the hallmarks of a profession is a university qualification as the entry standard. While there has been a long-standing debate as to whether social work is considered a profession along the same lines as medicine and law, there is no doubt that one of the strategies used to promote professionalization has been the establishment of social work degrees. During the twentieth century, universities, with their scientific and philosophical traditions, were seen to give status to rising professions, such as social work. Today, social work education is offered at qualifying level through both undergraduate (bachelor's) and post-graduate (master's) degrees. Advanced studies in social work are also offered through a wide range post-qualifying certificates, diplomas, master's degrees and doctorates.

However, universities don't just offer status to social work. They also offer structures, processes, cultures and theory that facilitate some key qualities, attributes and competencies in social work practitioners. In addition to providing access to relevant knowledge, universities assist the development of core skills, such as critical thinking, the capacity to theorize, the ability to develop and use research, and skills in written and verbal communication. The diversity of the benefits gained from university education can be appreciated by perusing the lists of learning outcomes and graduate attributes that universities promote as being achieved on the completion of a course or degree programme.

But things haven't always gone smoothly. Over the years there have been regular debates about the appropriateness of university-based programmes for preparing social work students for practice. Concerns have been expressed about splits between theory and practice, and between the university and the 'real world'. While both of these critiques can be challenged, it is, nonetheless, the case that more and more effort is going into ensuring that, as well as providing intellectually challenging environments, universities deliver programmes that meet the requirements of the industry and the end users of social work services – service users, clients and community members.

In countries such as the UK and Australia, governments, regulatory bodies and professional associations are placing increasing demands on universities to ensure that they graduate students who are 'job ready'. For example, in the UK more emphasis is being placed on ensuring that social work education contains significant amounts of practice learning and is focused on the needs and concerns of service users. Practice competence is also facilitated by having the National Occupational Standards for Social Work underpin the social work curriculum. These standards set the benchmark for good practice and students are required to meet and demonstrate these standards by the time that they complete their degree. The purpose of social work and the key roles are outlined below. A full copy of the National Occupational Standards can be accessed from the Skills for Care website, listed at the end of this chapter.

Purpose and key roles of social work

The National Occupational Standards (Topss, 2002) outline the following purpose of social work, based on a definition by the International Association of Schools of Social Work and the International Federation of Social Workers:

> [Social work is] a profession which promotes social change, problem solving in human relationships and the empowerment and liberation of people to enhance well-being. Utilising theories of human behaviour and social systems, social work intervenes at the points where people interact with their environments. Principles of human rights and social justice are fundamental to social work. (Topss, 2002: 12)

From this definition a series of key roles were developed:

> Key Role 1: Prepare for, and work with individuals, families, carers, groups and communities to assess their needs and circumstances.
> Key Role 2: Plan, carry out, review and evaluate social work practice, with individuals, families, carers, groups, communities and other professionals.
> Key Role 3: Support individuals to represent their needs, views and circumstances.
> Key Role 4: Manage risk to individuals, families, carers, groups, communities, self and colleagues.
> Key Role 5: Manage and be accountable, with supervision and support, for your own social work practice within your organisation.
> Key Role 6: Demonstrate professional competence in social work practice. (Topss, 2002: 12)

In Australia, the Australian Association of Social Workers (AASW) has rolled out strategies to ensure that universities increase students' competence in child protection, mental health work, cross-cultural practice, and work with Indigenous Australians. These developments rightly challenge universities – and their staff – to stay actively engaged with developments in social work practice, and in other areas such as social policy and the law.

For new students, universities can seem like large, impersonal, arcane bureaucracies. While this may be true to some extent, it is the case that universities are, fundamentally, human organizations. They rely substantially on their human resources to deliver their services, and the products of their industry are human qualities, such as increased knowledge and skills. And they are very much human in their politics, their mistakes and their struggles over funding and access to other resources. In this sense, universities are not so dissimilar to the organizations social workers work in: they are often under-resourced, dealing with complex issues, and negotiating with their students/clients through webs of power-based relationships. But, also like social work organizations, they are made up of people who are passionate about what they do, who want to promote goals such as freedom to learn and to speak out, and who want to make a difference in society. This is certainly the case for many social work academics. As one second year social work student said:

> *A lot of teachers teach because they love social work and they want us to have the best knowledge that we can. They are teaching because they love the occupation. (SW student)*

CHALLENGES FOR NEW SOCIAL WORK STUDENTS

As large and complex organizations, universities present many challenges for new students, including new social work students. These challenges affect the capacity of students to study and prepare themselves for professional practice. Many students in qualifying social work programmes, at both undergraduate and post-graduate levels, are mature-age and are entering university after a period in the workforce. This can be daunting and these students inevitably require assistance getting back into the swing of writing assignments and preparing for exams. For younger students, it quickly becomes apparent that university is not like school, and there are fewer people around to actively check up to see you are doing the work and meeting your responsibilities. Both groups will need to become more confident with the style of writing and presenting expected in a university setting as this may differ considerably from what they have been used to.

> *Improve timekeeping … Keep diary … Meet deadlines. (SW student; O'Connor et al., 2009: 443)*

For many students, a key challenge is balancing the different commitments they have in their life. Academics often reflect wistfully on the days when university education was free, when attendance was high in classes, and when people had time to participate in student politics. While the latter two are certainly still achievable (and desirable), it is nonetheless the case that today's students have more and more demands placed on their time. Time to work to survive, time spent on family and parenting responsibilities, and time for leisure all compete with time available for study. We discuss these issues in depth in Chapter 2, but it's worth noting here that developing positive time management and self care strategies at university will stand you in good stead after graduation as these are also big issues in social work practice.

One important matter that confronts many new students is negotiating computer and IT (information technology) systems. While the media spends a lot of energy dissecting the latest internet developments and fads, it is important to recognize that not everyone feels comfortable with accessing the latest technology. But to be an effective social work student it is essential to come to grips with some key resources. These include electronic library catalogues, which enable you to search for and access library resources, as well as online databases which help you search large numbers of journal abstracts to find the latest material on a particular topic (discussed further in Chapter 3). E-mail will become for most a primary means of communication with academic staff and fellow students, and web-based educational tools (such as Blackboard or Moodle) are widely used in most universities. And internet-based social media (such as Facebook and Twitter) are quickly becoming frontline resources, particularly in the provision of informal support and friendship, which help people survive and thrive in university life.

> I think you need to have a few friends around at uni that know where you're at and know where they're at. [Knowing that] we are all in the same place normalizes without everyone going crazy at the same time. So you need to have that kind of community help. (SW student)

Two other key challenges for new students are feeling comfortable in expressing personal views and knowing how and when to stand up for one's rights. It is a sad reality that some students go through university without having a single meaningful one-to-one conversation with a university lecturer. While this is probably less likely in social work than in some other disciplines, it is true that many find it difficult speaking up in class or approaching academic staff. This is particularly so for those students for whom English is not their first language or who have communication difficulties (e.g. because of anxiety). Effective communication with academics is critical when problems are encountered, such as when you feel you have been unfairly treated or discriminated against. Being able to talk directly to the person concerned is usually the first step in conflict management processes within universities and is, coincidentally, a basic social work skill. There are other ways of providing feedback (e.g. through course evaluations), and making concerns heard (e.g. via anti-discrimination officers, and the support of student unions).

> We needed some guidance, everyone was anxious, it was the first assignment, didn't have clue and when we were saying, 'look we need help here', it was like 'oh you need to take responsibility, you need to be reading'. What do we need to be reading? We need some structure. (SW student; Worsley et al., 2009: 834)

> I came to uni really under prepared. I had never done academic writing before. (SW student)

For most social work students, the key challenge will be developing studying skills – researching and writing assignments, developing skills in critical analysis, and conducting presentations. These challenges are the focus of our book. In many ways they are about how to develop and present effectively your own knowledge for professional social work. Before overviewing each of the chapters, some important points in relation to the development of knowledge for professional social work practice are highlighted.

KNOWLEDGE FOR PROFESSIONAL PRACTICE

DIFFERENT SOURCES OF KNOWLEDGE

Social work draws on a wide range of disciplines and practices from psychology to organizational management, from social policy to community development: it is truly a transdisciplinary profession. So in thinking about how to study for social work, it is important to recognize that there are different types or sources of knowledge you will draw upon in professional practice. When thinking about knowledge you might automatically think about 'facts' or evidence, or alternatively about theories. And everyone involved in social work has a view on what sorts of knowledge you need in order to be an effective practitioner. Social workers in the field may highlight the value of common sense knowledge that is applied in specific practice situations. Service users may value knowledge of local resources. Managers may emphasize knowledge of organizational policies and procedures. Funders may prioritize knowledge gained through an evaluation of the effectiveness of professional intervention. Academics may emphasize practice theories and broader theoretical perspectives to help inform and critique practice.

While this is a caricature of what managers, practitioners, and others might prioritize in social work knowledge, it does highlight the different sources of knowledge that are drawn upon in practice. According to Drury Hudson (1997), social work professional knowledge comprises:

- *Empirical knowledge:* knowledge drawn from the findings of research studies based on a range of different methodologies, but usually incorporating quantitative and/or qualitative methods.
- *Procedural knowledge:* knowledge about organizational policies and procedures, as well as government policy and legislative requirements.
- *Practice wisdom:* knowledge gained from practice experience that develops over time – it emerges from a sense of having previously encountered similar practice situations.
- *Personal knowledge:* intuitive and common sense knowledge that you have gained by being part of a particular culture or society.
- *Theoretical knowledge:* knowledge of a range of different theories that can be used to inform and critique practice; this can include broad orienting theories (e.g. sociological and psychological theories), as well as more specific practice theories and models (e.g. anti-oppressive practice; the strengths perspective).

These are not discrete sets of knowledge. For example, a child welfare agency may have organizational procedures that reinforce an anti-racist practice (see Turney, 1997) and a strengths-based approach (see Saleebey, 2008) to working with young people; or research findings on the reluctance of older people to question medical practitioners' advice may coalesce with your practice experience in hospital discharge planning. However while each source of knowledge may reinforce another source, they may also be in conflict and be used to interrogate each other. For example, a practitioner's personal value that people should not have sex before marriage may be challenged by a disability support agency's policy that enables clients to establish sexual relationships and with research that demonstrates the positive impact of such relationships on people's quality of life. Similarly, the value of a particular practice model might be brought into question by research findings which suggest that the model is less effective than other intervention methods.

While university study tends to highlight the importance of empirical, theoretical, and procedural knowledge, in social work degrees there is recognition of the need to develop practice experience and wisdom and of understanding how personal knowledge affects practice. So it is necessary to think carefully about these sources of knowledge and how they can be made use of in different practice situations. Throughout this book we recognize the value of learning about and within these different sources of knowledge. We turn now to a brief discussion of two threshold concepts: evidence-based practice and critical reflective practice.

EVIDENCE-BASED PRACTICE

One of the key challenges in professional practice is being able to make use of the wide range of knowledge and information to inform the work. Evidence-based practice (EBP) is an approach to the use of research to inform social workers' work and decision making. Increasingly social work degree programmes and government agencies are highlighting the importance of this approach. EBP was originally developed in relation to medicine as a means of better informing clinicians' treatment decisions. In social work the approach involves evaluating the quality of research findings (e.g. by evaluating how successfully the methodology employed helps answer the research questions) and using that information to inform practice decisions. According to a report prepared for the Social Care Institute for Excellence (Marsh and Fisher, 2005: 3), 'evidence = research findings + interpretation of the findings'. EBP has been promoted as a means of overcoming professional authority (i.e. the professional knows best) by ensuring that clients are offered the most effective intervention (i.e. what works best).

As in medicine and nursing, EBP has been substantially debated within social work. Key concerns relate to the alignment of evidence-based practice with managerialist demands for practitioners to demonstrate their cost effectiveness. Thus some practitioners have been concerned that EBP can erode professional autonomy. Others have been concerned about its focus on guiding professional decision making – arguing that the rational and logical approach to EBP decision making does not reflect the complex reality of how most decisions are made (Webb, 2001). Others highlight the potential for clients and service users to be left out of the decision making altogether, reinforcing rather than reducing professional authority and control (Beresford and Evans, 1999). Also within social work there have been concerns that some types of research evidence (e.g. that produced via experimental designs) tend to be valued more highly than others (e.g. that arising from qualitative studies) and that this may not always be appropriate. Increasingly social workers are thinking more broadly about what constitutes evidence, and how research evidence is only one source of knowledge informing practice (e.g. alongside service user preferences). In this way, the emphasis in social work is often on 'research-mindedness' in the sense that a range of appropriate research knowledge should be drawn upon routinely in practice situations. Thus for both students and practitioners it is critically important to understand how research is carried out and how to evaluate it. We explore these issues in depth in Chapter 5.

CRITICAL REFLECTIVE PRACTICE

Another approach to thinking about knowledge in professional practice which you are likely to encounter early on in a social work degree is critical reflective practice. While critical reflective practice looks at knowledge in a different way from EBP, the ideas are not necessarily incompatible. However, whereas EBP emphasizes the application of knowledge (particularly research knowledge) to practice situations, critical reflective practice seeks mainly to generate knowledge from practice experiences. That is, its focus is on how practitioners (and students) reflect critically on their practice and then continue to refine and improve their practice based on this understanding. A similar concept is reflective practice and the two terms may be used interchangeably by some. However, as noted below, for us the use of the term 'critical' signifies the importance of understanding power relations and the need to promote equitable relationships both within social work and within society more widely as well as of the centrality of anti-oppressive practices.

According to Hughes and Heycox (2010) critical reflective practice can be seen to comprise four inter-related dimensions: reflective learning, emotionality, criticality, and reflexivity. Reflective learning relates to the process of purposely and carefully thinking before, during, and after action (e.g. an interview with a client) about the experience and how your understanding of the situation is developing. Schön's (1983) concept of the 'reflective practitioner' embodies the idea of 'reflection on action', during which practitioners reflect on how they made sense of a particular situation and what they can learn from it.

Emotionality refers to the importance of staying in tune with and critiquing the emotional dimensions of professional encounters. The literature on psychodynamic practice and observation is useful here in highlighting the importance of practitioners attending to the emotional undercurrents in practice (Briggs, 1999). An understanding of other people's and one's own emotions is an important source of information in professional practice. For example, understanding and responding to the emotional climate of a support group the first time a new member attends is an important function in group work facilitation. Similarly, understanding your own, sometimes negative, emotional responses (e.g. of like or dislike) when encountering a client for the first time is essential to ensure you provide a good quality service to all people.

The concept of criticality, as discussed, relates to an understanding of how power is reflected in social work relationships and more widely within society. Thus, in this context, being critical does not just mean being analytical, it also means being able to expose inequality, oppression, and disadvantage. This understanding of criticality is informed by critical social theory, involving the application to social work of ideas and values from areas such as anti-oppressive practice, feminism, political economy theory, critical disability studies, decolonization and postmodernism. In line with some of the radical and structural traditions in social work, critical reflective practice would also involve recognition of the need for action as well as critique (Adams, 2002). That is, social work practitioners (and students) must use their understanding of power and inequality to inform community and social action that tries to redress such injustices.

Reflexivity has been defined in different ways (D'Cruz et al., 2007), but includes the idea that knowledge is constantly folding back and emerging as you subject yourself and others to critical scrutiny. In particular, what is emphasized is the need to examine one's own identities, values, attitudes and beliefs and how these impact on your understanding of and action in practice situations. It involves developing an awareness of self and of how this sense of self impacts on your work. For example, how does a heterosexual man's sense of his self and his sexual and gender identity impact on his work with other heterosexual men and women, and with gay and lesbian people? This self awareness has long been a feature within social work through the popularization of the concept 'use of self' in the sense of how we use our bodies, knowledge and skills to form effective professional relationships. Particularly relevant is an understanding of self as constructed through relationships and interactions, and as being in constant development (Arnd-Caddigan and Pozzuto, 2008).

Some of these ideas are discussed further in Chapter 4 where a range of issues in relation to learning for professional practice are discussed. Social work degrees are not just about instilling knowledge in students, but also about developing your own capacity to generate and access knowledge to inform your professional work.

OVERVIEW OF THE BOOK

The topics presented in this book reflect our own experiences as students, as well as our experiences as teachers and academic advisors. They are informed by comments and feedback we have received from social work students in focus groups and have gathered from reports of social work students' experience in the UK and Australia. Our aim is to help you identify and develop the appropriate skills to survive and thrive at university. We talk broadly of 'study skills', but these extend beyond simply studying for exams. They also include knowing how to write appropriately for an academic context, how to think critically, how to manage time effectively, how to access information, and how to present well. All of these skills are transferable to social work practice. Being able to write for a range of audiences is essential. Thinking critically and analytically is key to improving the quality of practice. Accessing information, including research knowledge, is crucial, as is being able to present effectively to a wide range of groups.

In order to gain the most from the learning opportunities available in social work programmes, students need to be well organized in terms of the use of their time

2 TIME: THE ELASTIC COMMODITY

In this chapter we look at your management of time as a social work student. It will help you to:

- understand how you make best use of time;
- plan your studying;
- deal with anxiety over deadlines and time pressure;
- recognize the different demands on your time as a social worker in the making.

The laws of science do not distinguish between the forward and backward directions of time. (Hawking, 1988: 160)

Time may be looped in the bizarre world of quantum physics but that is not the case for you – time marches ever forward for the social work student. Time is tricky and needs management. But Hawking (1988) following Einstein also demonstrated that time is relative and malleable, and by clever planning you can 'create' time for your study as well as your personal needs.

Remember when you were young and Christmas or your birthday was just taking forever to come around whereas when they did at last arrive, time seemed to speed up and they were gone in a flash. In other words, time is a dimension in your life that is subject to your perception and your management.

A MATTER OF ETHICAL PRACTICE

Social work practice can be pressured and require strong organisation of time and good analytical skills in clarifying and taking in large amounts of information. (SW student; O'Connor et al., 2009: 442)

Good time management is a professional social work obligation. The IFSW (2004), AASW (2002), BASW (2002) and NASW (1996), in fact, all social work codes of ethics implicitly and explicitly require social workers to manage their time to the benefit of their clients, their employer, and the profession as a whole. This is because these codes demand that the profession is practised with competence and account-ability to 'the users of their services, the people they work with, their colleagues, their employers, the professional association' (IFSW 2004). So you, as an emerging social worker, can best develop this 'good use of time' skill whilst studying for social work because many of the time issues are the same for students and practising social workers. For example, case management requires planning ahead, juggling compet-ing time demands, being on time, preparing well before each meeting or session, being ready to manage unexpected demands and setting target dates or times for completion of tasks or aspects of the case plan in a similar manner to managing study tasks. It is respectful, a key social work value, to spend the time necessary to do the best for the persons with whom you are working but also to close off the work when appropriate so that others can be treated with the same respect.

PLANNING YOUR TIME

Planning is fundamental to managing your time. This involves:

- knowing what your study tasks are;
- knowing when tasks are due;
- prioritising tasks according to their importance.

But useful planning also depends upon:

- knowing yourself;
- knowing how you work;
- knowing what motivates you;
- what will work for you.

Social work students often have heavier class and assignment loads than those studying for a general arts or science degree, as a social work degree has a tightly packed curriculum of professionally prescribed skills, knowledge and theory as well as block field practice learning and experience to cover. So time management for you involves high-level organizational ability that, as noted above, is also essential for you as a social worker. Don't worry if you don't have this skill yet – it can be learnt.

First, get to know how you work best in the academic environment. Knowing yourself is another social work principle that should become part of your life as a student. This is covered in part in Chapter 4 but there are specific aspects of knowing yourself in relation to managing your time that you can consider.

Some students need to start working on an assignment weeks ahead, otherwise their level of anxiety becomes a negative factor:

I have to start early to read for an assignment or prepare for a presentation or an exam otherwise I panic. If I start early I feel at least I've broken the ice. (SW student)

This student knows he will become panic stricken and thus unable to work effectively if he doesn't make an early start, an acknowledgement that the truism that writing the first word or reading the first article early, 'breaking the ice', is a vital part of a successful time management strategy.

Others work better if they start closer to the due date:

> I guess it depends on your personality. If I start too early I just stress because I keep changing and reworking it. It's much better if I do it closer to when it's due then I don't keep worrying about what I've already written. (SW student)

This student knows she's a bit of a perfectionist and will not gain any benefit, but in fact will become more stressed by starting too early. This doesn't mean she starts the night before of course, but means she starts with enough time, knowing her own working style, to draft and rework the draft ready for the due date.

The important point here is that you plan according to what you know will get the tasks done in time and at the highest intellectual level possible for you.

Try answering the questions below to build your knowledge of how you handle time.

Knowing myself in relation to time management

1. In what circumstances do I produce my best work? For example, under pressure; with plenty of lead time; working steadily; in short intense bursts.
2. Am I a procrastinator? (so need to take the first step, set myself strict timelines and stick to them)
3. Am I often running late? (so need to reorganize my time to make sure I am on time)
4. Am I often running early? (so am well organized and can capitalize on that)
5. Am I a perfectionist? (so need to set time limits on my study tasks)

Try self-observing over the next week or two; ask friends and family how they observe you to learn more about how you deal with time. Look at how you manage it in different circumstances, for instance, how you deal with looming deadlines, conflicting priorities, people who 'get in the way' of completing required tasks.

CLEVER USE OF TIME

> ... do the reading first, before I went to the lecture and it at least gave me some sort of grounding, some sort of, at least a few buzz words and maybe the general sort of thing they're talking about, without making really, really comprehensive sense out of it. And then it'd make a lot more sense as I went to the lecture. (SW student)

Of course assignments are only a part of your study time commitment. Assessment tasks can be made easier by doing a number of other study tasks regularly. The following are simple but effective steps to take before and after classes to set you up well for doing your assignments. Build these steps into your study routine:

Preparation and review time

1. Prepare for seminars, tutorials, and lectures by doing the set readings and making notes and summaries and thinking about the topic.
2. Prepare properly for practical classes, that is ensure you know where this practice (such as interviewing skills) fits into preparing to be a social worker, what the theories that underpin it are and what the nature of the particular practice is.
3. Review your lecture and seminar notes after each session or at least weekly.

These three activities, although seemingly time consuming and perhaps initially thought of as a nuisance, will prove time efficient in the long run. This is because your brain works to synthesize information and knowledge as you gather it (Gross, 1999) and the more you help that process along the way rather than by trying to do it at the last minute, the better your grasp of the field of study, the more holistic your understanding and the quicker you can pull together a coherent and cohesive account of that knowledge and practice both for final assessments and for professional practice. This is in harmony with the well-established principle that breaking your learning or study into chunks (Zerubavel, 1999) is beneficial. It allows you to process the work in your brain, gives you regular physical breaks and makes the whole task seem doable rather than an unscaleable mountain; tackle the mountain sections at a time. You can also reward yourself when you've completed that chunk (Field et al., 1989).

WAYS OF PLANNING

Some form of list making and then prioritizing the items on the list are basic planning tools that you may have brought with you to university but, if you didn't, then now is the time to make them part of your basic management repertoire.

My advice is to make lists and allocate time to yourself to do them. (SW student)

Listing the study tasks you have to do over the next month, two months, and semester (short, medium, and long-term) is essential to ensuring you get them all done. There is the added bonus of feeling a sense of pride, relief and accomplishment as you tick them off the list.

Prioritizing things on the list is the next step. Knowing how to prioritize is an essential social work skill, as there will always be competing demands on your time and people will be depending upon you to deal with matters according to their importance. You may have a regular appointment with a family, at the same time an urgent call comes in from another family that they are in crisis and you also have a deadline looming for a briefing paper for your supervisor. The decision as to what to prioritize amongst these depends upon your professional and skilled judgement of the circumstances of each of the matters at hand. Honing this kind of professional judgment starts during your university years.

Prioritizing your social work study tasks applies internally:

> *For all assessments it's important to look at the weightings assigned to each one or even each part of an assignment. If for instance it says this is worth 20 per cent and this is worth 40 per cent then you should spend more time on the 40 bit. (SW student)*

as well as prioritizing choices between tasks. For example, in a choice between reading for an essay due in four weeks and preparing a seminar presentation to be given in two weeks, the presentation preparation comes first. To do this kind of prioritizing you need to have a long term list so you can see the whole picture and not be caught out at the last minute with, say three assignments due close together.

Some aspects of study can be time eaters if you let them:

> *On the other hand using online learning like being in an online discussion that is being counted towards your final mark is very time consuming. It eats into your time more than other forms of learning because it's always there and you're expected to take part and know what everyone else has said. It can take up hours. So you need to manage time well and need to establish with the tutor just what's expected. (SW student)*

Many courses have online learning or e-learning as an integral aspect of the course requirements. Learning how to use online tutorials and discussions efficiently is a skill in itself. Such a learning environment is seductive, just as playing virtual games, blogging, twittering and joining in a chat room can be all engaging activities in which you can lose track of time. Ensure you know the requirements and that you do not give such e-learning sessions more time than is necessary or appropriate. It's also important to talk to your lecturer or tutor about the time involved if the commitment you are devoting to it is more than seems reasonable.

Use your practicum time as well to build your skill in prioritizing. Discuss your priority listings and use of time with your practice teacher or supervisor to test whether you are developing the skills needed and seek feedback about whether you are making the right calls in relation to prioritizing: whether you are spending enough or too much time on your tasks.

USING A PLANNER

Because a social work degree contains a wide range of learning and teaching forms: in assessment tasks, from essays to presentations, exams to evaluation of practice skills; and in other forms of learning from lectures to group work, practicum to field visits, you cannot necessarily rely on the regular rhythm your old school or many other degrees or work places maintain.

Using a yearly planner is an excellent way to organize in the long term and to plan for these different, sometimes irregular patterns of learning.

I have a wall planner that is fantastic. I put all the important dates on it and it sits on the wall in the hallway and I check it all the time so there are no surprises. (SW student)

Write the dates when all assignments are due and exams are scheduled. You may find it helpful to draw lines back from the due dates to the date you plan to start working on the task. You could colour code for different courses.

But you will also need to have shorter term planning such as on a weekly basis. A diary with time blocked out for classes and seminars, work, and sporting or other regular commitments is essential. Remember that a social work course may contain field visits, such as a half or full day visit to a prison or a community centre, scattered over the semester and you need to log them into your diary and planner as soon as they are announced so that you can plan around that unusual time commitment. You can then see what time you have for study and match that with the tasks on the planner.

It's also important to plan your university work and study realistically according to your personal circumstances. You may have health or disability needs that require both planned and unplanned attention or you may be a carer. Make sure you take advantage of any university supports if you are in this circumstance as this will also save you time in the long run.

Whatever your circumstances, plan to meet the expected and unexpected time requirements:

I try to plan blocks of study time but I have a young child so have to study whenever I can. (SW student)

MANAGING STUDY STRESS BY MANAGING YOUR TIME WELL

Time stress can be created internally or externally. You can create your own stress by not planning well, procrastinating, or looking at your work as one huge task rather than as in manageable sections. You can also be time stressed by unexpected personal or paid work requirements, financial problems, accidents or ill health. You can mitigate these by being as well organized and prepared as possible and using preventive approaches to stress-creating circumstances. Bradley (1992) proposed stress and time management workshops for qualifying social workers and these would be an excellent addition to the curriculum. But in their absence learning for yourself stress management methods whilst at university, that suit you, from exercise to meditation, is a wonderful gift to yourself that will be as beneficial when you are a practising social worker as when a student.

Stress management tips

1. Take regular activity breaks: exercising or just getting active, such as a brisk walk, taking the dog for a run, or some stretches, boosts endorphin levels that make you feel good and positive. A ten-minute meditation break can do the same thing.
2. Keep up regular sport or other activity such as dancing a few times a week. This provides longer-term physical and mental balance.
3. Go to sleep before you get too tired. This wards off stress related exhaustion. But if you are stressed and can't get to sleep, try deep breathing, meditation, and positive self-talk. Set yourself a routine bedtime with activities beforehand to help you unwind: music, massage.
4. Eating nutritious food like fresh fruit and vegetables, cereals, grains, nuts and proteins and drinking plenty of water are good for your brain and blood sugar levels and in turn assist to reduce stress. Enjoy your meals – don't eat and try to work at the same time.
5. Be social. You tend to do better if you are connected with others. So build social activities with family and friends into your timetable.
6. Join or create a study group. By working cooperatively with a small group of your peers you multiply the chances of covering study points and issues as well as reducing stress. And you feel good because you're helping each other.
7. Ask your tutor, the student support officers, or your friends for help when you need it. You know the old saying: 'a stitch in time …'.

All these 'tips' are as relevant to you as a professional social worker and as a student.
(with acknowledgement to: http://www.studentservices.uwa.edu.au/ss/learning/studying_smarter/jump_start/managing_study_stress)

MAKE USE OF THE TIME OTHERS OFFER

Make the best use of the instantly available online library information systems. It is the most efficient use of your time to learn, early on in your degree, how to use these systems specifically for social work knowledge gathering. Most universities have tutorials for different disciplines and provide social work specific information packages.

Logging onto the uni library data bases and having instant access to information is amazing. (SW student)

Your lecturers and supervisors set aside time for consultation. Make use of that.

Next semester I want to make better use of the teacher consultation times. (SW student)

Make an appointment and go with your list of questions and concerns. It will save you anxiety and confusion and thus time, if you clarify content, practice issues, or theory questions sooner rather than later. You may also find, as do many students, that devoting time to a study circle or group with your peers pays enormous dividends.

STUDY-LIFE BALANCE

Work-life balance is important to me – getting it balanced. Make time for leisure and relaxation. (SW student)

Social workers should practise what they preach. To improve well-being they promote a balanced life to those with whom they work and should try to maintain such a practice themselves.

You may feel you don't have time to relax or spend time with friends or family or pursue sport or a hobby, but that is a false economy. There is ample evidence that you will gain greater satisfaction from and do well in your study if you make time for friends and for the things that matter to you. Researchers found that, amongst other things, social support and balance of life and work roles were important in students' life satisfaction (Sturhahn Stratton et al., 2006). This is supported by students we interviewed:

Spend time with others on the SW degree but don't neglect your other friends. Makes you feel good and if you feel good you do better in your degree. It helps you study. (SW student)

The operative idea here is balance. Obviously if you spend too much time socializing you won't learn and won't graduate, but if you study obsessively to the neglect of the rest of your being you may not develop into a well-grounded and rounded social worker, the kind of social worker who brings a personal understanding of the importance, and has the skill of managing time to achieve beneficial results for self and others.

Here is a final word. Being obsessive about time management can be as bad as never meeting deadlines. It has been argued that some of the more recent time management systems are over-the-top (Abrahamson and Freedman, 2007). Some people spend a lot of money on time coaching with more time being spent on making lists and getting organized and less on actually getting the work done. Again balance appears to be the operative concept. So try out some of the approaches suggested and come up with your own way of managing your time best.

CONCLUSION

Key aspects of time management for social work students have been examined in this chapter. We have highlighted the importance of you knowing yourself and how you work best under time constraints. For those of you who experience anxiety about academic work we suggest careful planning and prioritization of your study tasks. A key to enjoying your time as a social work student is to acknowledge other aspects of your life and allow space and time to ensure work-life balance.

Finding out more

Websites

All universities have student support centers that provide study time management advice and it is well worth checking out your university's student support web page. Here are just a handful of examples to get you started.

The Learn Higher Centre for Excellence in Teaching and Learning has an excellent summary of study time management skills and tips:
http://www.learnhigher.ac.uk/learningareas/timemanagement/home.htm

The University of Manchester's study skills page has a range of practical advice and activities to help you manage your time:
http://www.humanities.manchester.ac.uk/studyskills/

The University of Queensland has a useful time and management study page under its learning banner on the student services page:
http://www.uq.edu.au/student-services/

The University of Western Australia Managing Student Stress web page is a most helpful expansion on the stress tips outlined in this chapter:
http://www.studentservices.uwa.edu.au/ss/learning/studying_smarter/jump_start/managing_study_stress

Reading

Levin, P. (2007) *Skilful Time Management.* Berkshire: Open University Press, McGraw-Hill.

3 MANAGING THE LITERATURE: LEARNING TO LOVE INFORMATION MANAGEMENT

In this chapter, we explore the different types of information you, as a social work student will access and make use of in your academic work. These include sources of information such as text books, journal articles, and scholarly books. The chapter aims to assist you to:

- manage literature;
- search for information;
- use information management technology;
- be discerning about using literature.

The problem is you do have so much information at your disposal. (SW student)

WHAT IS THIS THING CALLED 'THE LITERATURE'?

Academic study employs terms mysterious to the uninitiated. 'The literature' is one of these. There is, for example, 'discipline literature', 'professional literature' as well as 'the literature search' and 'the literature review'.

'Literature' is the body of information published in some form or other, on a particular topic, area of study, discipline or profession that is the result of someone else's research, observation, and analysis. Depending upon the topic, 'literature' can encompass journal articles, scholarly books, research and other reports, text books, documentaries and electronic publications. These works provide considered summaries, thoughts and analyses in an area of interest, and provide you with knowledge and perspectives on a topic or area of your study. Your courses have reading lists that represent a small part of the literature that your lecturer considers important in that area of study. Social work literature encompasses a broader range of information than most, because social work draws on such a wide range of disciplines, theories, and practices, from the sociological to the psycho-social, from policy to research methods, from counselling to ethics.

'The literature' is distinct from primary sources, research information, and data that a researcher gathers. You may, for example, interview people (with ethics approval of course), who have been going to a social work service like a community centre, as part of a study project on that centre. The transcriptions of those interviews are not literature. They are 'raw' data or information that you will then analyse and report on (discussed further in Chapter 5). The written report that you make, if it is published in some reviewed form, may then, in the future, become part of 'the literature' in that field for other people to use.

WHY LITERATURE IS IMPORTANT

Your lecturers use literature as a foundational aspect of their teaching. It provides both historical and contemporary knowledge and thinking in a field.

Take a course on working with groups. One or more text books may be required reading, with a supplementary list for each week's topic such as the history of group work, theories informing working with groups, values, approaches, working with voluntary and involuntary groups and so on. Your lecturer will have provided introductory readings but also have framed the course around particular approaches to working with groups informed by her reading of the literature as well as by her own practice and primary research. If you don't read some of that literature, you won't know what has already been understood, discussed, debated, researched and agreed, or is still contested. Your lecturers will expect you to become familiar with the foundational literature in the different areas of social work study, so that you have a base upon which to develop your own thinking and practice. But more than that, you are expected, from the beginning of your social work degree, to complete assignments using and referring to the literature to advance your discussion and arguments. If you have an assignment on current issues in child protection or on housing policies addressing social inequality you would need to use the library databases (these are discussed later in this chapter) to find relevant literature to inform you of the main debates and theories and to search for current government and departmental reports in these fields before writing your assignment.

MANAGING THE LITERATURE AS AN ETHICAL PRACTICE

If you don't inform yourself of what is being done, thought, researched, and proposed in social work, you will not be an ethical social worker.

All social work codes of ethics, including the International Federation of Social Workers (IFSW), demand that social workers keep their theory and practice knowledge up to date. The British Association of Social Workers' code requires that social workers identify and disseminate knowledge and skills (3.5.2:1) and similarly the Australian Association of Social Workers' code expects that they will appraise new approaches and methodologies to extend their professional expertise (4.1.5:d). Gaining skills in literature searching and management from the beginning of your social work degree will enable you to meet these social work professional expectations.

TYPES OF LITERATURE

So what are the types of literature you're being asked to find, read, understand, and organize?

As noted, social work traverses a wide range of knowledge, research, and practice streams and although all of these are integrated into the professional practice of social work, the literature in these areas is scattered across a variety of literature types. Wallace and Wray (2006: 17–20) divide literature into support and front line literature with textbooks, readers, handbooks and encyclopaedias in the former and theoretical books and those resulting from original research, reports, accounts of current practice, and policy statements in the latter category. Most social work students in the earlier years of their degree will rely heavily on support literature while building up to a greater familiarity with and use of front-line literature in their senior years. Although most books are still in hard copy form, increasingly all forms of literature are becoming available online so we will explore online material a little later. But whether online or not, the following are types of literature you will need to use.

SUPPORT LITERATURE

TEXT BOOKS

Text books are usually written by academics and practitioners who have a strong grasp of the literature, ideas, approaches and challenges in their fields and who make these accessible to students by synthesizing and summarizing this information and providing key references for follow up. On the whole, text books are introductory to an area of study, and are often titled as 'handbook of' or 'introduction to' or just by the name of the area, like 'social policy' or 'sociology' and have reputable publishers. Use them to open up an area of study and to give you the main concepts and theories as well as to explain the specialist terms in that field. They are also helpful guides in their reference lists, to more detailed and focused literature, like journal articles and scholarly books that you can use to follow up an aspect of particular interest.

READERS

The readers are amazing. (SW student)

Your social work course coordinator may put together a reader for the course or refer you to a reader published commercially. A reader is a compilation of journal articles, book chapters, and other appropriate writing relevant to that particular course. Readers can be valuable sources of literature because they represent, grouped together, key writers and thinkers and important documents in that field.

Use them in your searches for other literature by looking for other work which an author you find helpful has published, or chasing publications referenced in one of the readings that sound particularly useful.

I use all my readers from other courses which is just awesome when you are ... like ... I know this, I've heard of this before (in a reader) and you can just continue to build that knowledge. That's great. (SW student)

ENCYCLOPAEDIAS

There are some excellent encyclopaedias covering social work and social theory that are edited by senior academics and provide concise information on almost all aspects of social work. Their main usefulness is in giving you a solid introduction to your investigations on a particular topic by defining it and providing key writers and concepts for deeper reading.

FRONT LINE LITERATURE

PEER REVIEWED JOURNAL ARTICLES

These are articles that have been written by academics, practitioners, or researchers (and sometimes social work students) reflecting upon a particular topic in a scholarly manner. These articles are submitted to a journal that sends them out to be reviewed by two or three academics or researchers in that field who scrutinize the paper, make suggestions, and judge whether it is well enough researched, argued, and written to be published in that journal. So when an article appears in such a journal, like the *British Journal of Social Work*, *Australian Social Work* or *International Social Work* to name but three generalist social work journals, you can be assured it has been reviewed and commented upon by experts in that discipline. Peer reviewed journals are the most common source of published research and using them will provide you with the latest developments in particular fields of study.

SCHOLARLY BOOKS

These are written by leading researchers, thinkers, and practitioners providing insights into their innovative theoretical and practice approaches. Such books are usually the distillation of a period of developmental thinking and research and sometimes herald a change in theory or practice direction in a field. Although you will get a summary of key theories and theorists in support literature, you will need to read the original works especially as you progress in your degree, to gain the skills to assess them critically for yourself, and situate them in your growing social work repertoire.

REPORTS

Government departments, parliamentary inquiries, research centres, non-government agencies, private organizations and academics all author reports on topics as disparate as welfare payments, effects of climate change on social development, youth offending and housing for older persons. Although not peer-reviewed like journal articles and scholarly books, these reports often provide excellent summaries of the most recent research and writing as well as useful policy recommendations, and are important sources of information. More care though does need to be taken in scrutinizing how the report has been drawn together to ensure the accuracy of some sections. For example, Parliamentary Inquiry reports might quote evidence given to the inquiry but that does not necessarily mean that the information has been verified. In the UK, one good source of reports on the latest developments in social work is the Social Care Institute for Excellence (SCIE). The SCIE aims to identify and distribute knowledge to inform good practice. Reports available on their website (www.scie.org.uk) include research briefings, systematic reviews of important literature, and practice guidelines in particular fields.

RESEARCH UNITS AND BUREAUS

Social work relies quite heavily on data gathered by bureaus of statistics and such like. The UK Statistics Authority, its Australian equivalent, the Australian Bureau of Statistics, along with similar national bodies in every country, provide important data on populations. They gather and crunch the figures on everything from birth and death rates to employment and business statistics, to detailed demographics in smaller areas like postcodes and local council areas. Much of this information is online (the general information) and in databases (more detailed and complicated data) that you can search in your university virtual library. There are specialist units as well, such as the Home Office Research Development Statistics Unit (in the UK), various Bureaus of Crime Statistics in Australian States, and the Australian Institute of Family Studies. All these units produce highly reliable validated analysed data that will make your task of getting the most recent as well as comparative quantitative information on your study topic fairly straightforward.

PUBLIC INTEREST DOCUMENTARIES

Some well researched and produced social documentaries can be groundbreaking in highlighting social problems or issues that are of relevance to social work. For example, the public broadcasters in many countries have a high standard of investigative journalism producing public interest documentaries for TV and radio on matters such as the poor standard of health care in some Indigenous Australian communities or the neglect of older pensioners in some housing estates in Britain.

So you have at your disposal a wide range of information, but how do you find precisely what you need?

STRATEGIES FOR CONDUCTING LITERATURE SEARCHES

What is the purpose of your literature search? Is it to broaden your knowledge for a tutorial discussion or to satisfy your own interest in an area your lecturer has mentioned? Is it for an assignment? What is the topic?

Be clear about the question you are asking or the topic you are researching because, as Alice found through the Looking Glass, when you don't know where you're going you're bound to end up somewhere you hadn't intended to be.

This is detective work. Sometimes you have to hunt around a little until you find the right starting point and sometimes you can follow trails from one book or article to another.

Tips for successful literature searching

Basic Steps:

- Know how to use information technology effectively. For example, do modules from the European Computer Driver Licence foundation. http://www.ecdl.com/publisher/index.jsp

- Know your topic — make sure you understand what you're being asked to do.

- Use your course recommended reading list or reader as a starting point.

- Peruse other texts in the online library catalogue or on the shelf with the same code as a book you have found helpful.

- Check out the reference list in books or articles already recommended or that you have found useful.

- Look up the most recent edition of an official encyclopaedia like *The Blackwell Encyclopaedia of Social Work* (Davies, 2000) – don't use Wikipedia other than as a possible lead to more reliable sources.

It may be that this is the level of information gathering needed for your purposes. For example, if you are asked to lead a tutorial discussion on anti-oppressive practice (based on a chapter in your text book or reader) the above steps would be adequate to provide you with an understanding of, and a range of views on anti-oppressive practice for such a presentation task.

But writing assignments usually requires more specific information, after you have started with the sources just discussed, and therefore a more detailed search.

GO ONLINE YOUNG SOCIAL WORKER!

Again your university library is the best place to start but this time you will be using databases and online resources. Libraries have face-to-face or virtual tutorials and assistance on how to search databases most effectively and most have a specific social work subject guide. You will find these invaluable so make sure you are acquainted with all the social work resources your library offers. Investing time in learning to use these early on in your degree and making sure you update these skills every year, will pay dividends many times over during your studies. Many students find these online resources provide most of their information needs.

I only use the Library online. (SW student)

WHAT IS A DATABASE?

University libraries purchase and provide online access to a large number of academic databases that allow staff and students to search for published documentary and creative material. Databases are available for virtually all disciplines and professions. These databases are searchable by keywords, subject, author, title, date and so on. They provide full citation information – author, date, title, publisher, journal volume and page numbers if appropriate – and increasingly full texts of journal and magazine or newspaper articles so that you can read them online or download and print them. E-books are also becoming more common – but be careful to check that an e-book has been through a proper publication and refereeing process and that it is not just someone's self-published work that has not been subject to expert scrutiny. If an e-book is available through a university library database it is likely to have been formally published. Academic databases are highly reliable and current sources of information.

… when you are writing a paper to sort of pull up a journal that was published like a month ago or two months ago – that is just such a nice feeling. (SW student)

But that doesn't mean, of course, that the content of every article you download from a database is 'right'. Everything must be subjected to critical analysis, as we emphasize throughout this book. Just because a famous social work professor wrote it does not mean you shouldn't subject it to your sharp inquiry.

HOW TO USE DATABASES

- Do the database training your library provides.
- Work out keywords for your search – you will learn how to do this in the online database training. Some students like to start with a narrow search:

  I use very, very specific words … sometimes you get a zero response and that's fine, then I move out from there (2nd year SW student).

- Others like to start with broad terms and refine down their search by successively limiting it. You can also search by author, allowing you to gather the work written by a particular theorist for example.
- Select a database or set of databases to search provided by your library. There are numerous databases relevant to social work, but by no means limited to:

  – social work abstracts;
  – social care online;
  – social sciences index;
  – family and society studies;
  – sociological abstracts;
  – social services abstracts;
  – ISI web of knowledge;
  – criminal justice abstracts;
  – expanded academic asap;
  – AGELINE;
  – PsycINFO.

- Once you have retrieved some articles, you need to assess their relevance. Reading the abstracts is usually the best way to do this because abstracts provide the key content allowing you to assess whether it is relevant to your needs.
- I read the abstracts. I go through and read the abstracts. (SW student)

Libraries also have access to national statistical databases mentioned earlier and these are an excellent source of highly reliable information.

OTHER PLACES TO FIND INFORMATION

Although you are likely to find most of the information you need via these steps, there is some that you may need to look for in specific places. Government and Parliamentary Inquiry and specialist units' reports may not always find their way into databases so a search of their websites is a good idea. Many of these are highly relevant to social workers. For example, if you were investigating deprivation in the UK, you might go to the Cabinet Office's Social Exclusion Task Force website (http://www.cabinetoffice.gov.uk/); or if you want to find information on an Indigenous Australian social justice issue you would, as well as searching the usual books and databases, go to the Aboriginal and Torres Strait Islander and Social Justice Commissioner's website (http://www.hreoc.gov.au/Social_Justice/index.html). Similarly, to gain access to Parliamentary Inquiry reports you need to go on to the particular parliamentary website.

WHAT ABOUT GOOGLING IT?

Most of us love Google or similar search engines because in an instant we have information on how to get to that address or how to buy that iPad. But many websites contain information that has not been checked, may be outdated, or may be someone's individual pet topic. There is no regulation of the world wide web so great caution needs to be exercised when using it for academic social work purposes. You may want to know what reflective practice is and google it. You are likely to come up with over 1,000,000 hits, the first of which is likely to be Wikipedia that may or may not have been posted by someone who knows what reflective practice is. Some of these links will be serious and academically sound, but many will be, quite frankly, rubbish. And you certainly don't have the time to sift through them all. That's not to say that googling something specific is not valuable because it may be the quickest way to get to a website (like the Social Exclusion Task Force site). Google Scholar is a reasonably reliable source, as it tends to find scholarly articles such as reviewed journal articles. It is though, far better to use the sources discussed above – the support and frontline literature that you can access via hardcopy or your online library.

KEEPING TRACK OF YOUR LITERATURE

If you search your library's databases you can keep a full record of all the texts you have used:

> The other thing is that I use the record thing on the Library search, … it has every book I have ever looked at so far. (SW student)

Most university libraries provide staff and students with access to a bibliographic data program like Endnote or Procite. In fact the most recent versions of Microsoft Word are designed to be Endnote compatible. These are bibliographic software packages that allow you to store, organize, and manage your references in a database. You can transfer some of your library database references directly into that program, and add other references that you did not get through an online library search, creating your own comprehensive bibliography. Using a bibliographic software is the best way to organize your references as it configures your reference list at the click of your mouse to the style of referencing you need to use, whether Harvard, APA, or some other style.

EVALUATING QUALITY OF LITERATURE

All sources of literature are not equal. We have already mentioned the problem with websites and ensuring publications you use have been reviewed. There is still another matter that you need to consider when deciding whether to use information or not.

DOES THE PUBLICATION DATE MATTER?

That depends. If you are trying to understand the most recent developments in theory, policy, or practice, then yes.

> My only concern with books is that I try to see if they might be dated. I got caught out with that in first year. (SW student)

This student thought he had found just the literature he needed but when he received his assignment back the marker had noted that he had used 1980s books to outline recent directions in practice. Do check the publication date especially for demographic information. If you are quoting the latest rates on those receiving support benefits or children being looked after, make sure they are the latest.

On the other hand if you are discussing feminism you may well refer to de Beauvoir's *The Second Sex* originally published in 1949, or if you are critiquing the use of prisons, Foucault's *Discipline and Punish* first published in 1975 is an important text.

Information management guide

First familiarize yourself with how to use your library: complete the online how to use the library modules; learn how to search for information and to use the social work subject workbooks and guides. Libraries have very helpful staff and resources so make sure you make full use of everything your library has to offer.

Set up your personal Endnote or Procite (or whatever information management and referencing tool your university provides) account so that you have, from the beginning, a detailed online record of all the information sources you use and make sure you keep recording all your bibliographic details on an ongoing basis.

Organize your personal information account by topics and assignments and annotate your references in the information referencing tool you are using, so that you can retrieve relevant sources easily.

Make your text book, your reader and/or the library social work subject workbook your first port of call as your guide to the best information sources for your study activities.

Clarify, by analysing the assignment question and the length required, what level of and how much information you need for each study/assignment requirement.

CONCLUSION

Learning how to find the information you need and then to organize it, are some of the secrets to being a successful social work student and eventually a knowledgeable, up-to-date social worker. These and knowing how to assess whether a piece of literature or other information source is pertinent to your learning needs, your assignment or your presentation are skills you can develop early in your degree and ones that will improve your time management, your critical analysis, and not least your marks.

Finding out more

Every university library has an information skills section. As an example here is the University of Bath's page:
http://www.bath.ac.uk/library/infoskills/

And most university libraries have subject guides. Here is the University of New South Wales' page as an example:
http://subjectguides.library.unsw.edu.au/

Key online information sources for social workers are the various national statistics portals. The following are the national pages for the UK and Australia:
http://www.statistics.gov.uk/
http://www.abs.gov.au/

4 LEARNING FOR PROFESSIONAL PRACTICE: A SOCIAL WORKER IN THE MAKING

In this chapter we examine some of the issues involved in learning to become a social worker and in learning for professional practice. We will explore:

- how you learn best;
- different learning styles;
- the value gained from learning with others;
- the importance of reflective learning;
- practice learning on field placements.

It's very helpful to think of yourself not as a student, but as a social worker in the making. (SW student)

The shift from thinking about yourself as a student to thinking about yourself as an emerging social worker, 'a social worker in the making', emphasizes the vitality of learning for professional practice. You are in charge of your learning. Learning is not something that happens to you; it is something you actively engage in. While universities provide you with learning opportunities, much of what you learn and how you learn is up to you.

Thinking about yourself as a social worker in the making also brings into focus a key outcome of professional learning: ensuring that the end users of your knowledge and skills – service users and community members – will receive a good quality service. In this way, social work learning is different from learning about, for example, mathematics or Victorian poetry. Social work learning involves an ethical commitment to benefit the people you will work with.

Social work learning is not just something that is accomplished while at university. It begins at university and continues throughout a social work career. Learning for social work is never fully completed. What is crucial is an open-hearted and genuine commitment to pursue knowledge to improve practice. This approach reflects an active responsibility – a preparedness to face up to the challenges and to improve ourselves – rather than a passive responsibility, which involves doing just the bare minimum needed to survive (Bovens, 1998).

LEARNING HOW YOU LEARN BEST

Awareness of self, your identities, values, prejudices, capacities and gaps in understanding, is central to effective social work practice. The notion of 'use of self' encapsulates the idea that social workers should have a high level of self awareness and be able to use themselves carefully and purposefully to the benefit of the people and communities they are working with. The taking on of a social work identity is often a reflexive process, in that what develops is a critical understanding of how being (or becoming) a social worker affects how you think about yourself and how you engage with other people.

> *You've got to know yourself. And as social work students we are taught to be self-reflective so we should know ourselves and how we study best and how we respond to stress and anxiety. (SW student)*

Social work degrees include a wide variety of activities to help you learn, such as assignments, classroom activities, practice simulations and reflective journals. Awareness of which of the different learning strategies you find most challenging can help you determine how much time to allocate to the activity or whether or not to seek assistance early on. As an adult learner you will also be in a position to set up your own learning strategies. For example, while on placement you will probably need to outline your own learning plan: identifying the ways in which your learning goals will be met and how you can demonstrate that these goals were achieved.

Learning styles questionnaires provide a useful starting point for thinking and talking about how you learn best. One of the most widely used is Honey and Mumford's (1986) inventory. Which of the following learning styles sits most comfortably with you?

Honey and Mumford's (1986) Learning Styles

1. *Activists:* these people tend to be focused on doing as a way of learning. They operate more in the 'here and now' and are open minded, flexible, and eager to explore new experiences.
2. *Reflectors:* tend to hold back from action, focusing more on observing events from a distance. They may be more cautious in reaching conclusions and, in making judgements, draw on a wide range of information.
3. *Theorists:* approach learning in a rational manner. They tend to value objective information and try to construct logical theories based on this information.
4. *Pragmatists:* focus on experimenting with new ideas to see how they apply in practice. They are very much concerned with practical problem-solving as a way of learning and improving practice.

You might find it useful to consider past learning experiences. For example, if you are going to be involved in a group learning activity, then it would be helpful to reflect on past experiences of groups, particularly if you had a bad experience. What went well? What didn't go well? How did the group's learning fit with your own learning? Did you find it difficult to keep up or did you feel slowed down by the group's progress? What would you do differently in terms of promoting your own learning if you had your time again? The aim of all of this is for you to be more in control of your learning agenda.

LEARNING WITH OTHERS

Collectivity is so helpful and important for social work students, because that's what you learn about – to do social work well – but also for getting through your degree. (SW Student)

Social work learning, like social work practice, is not an isolated activity. Early on in your degree you are expected to work in groups, present in front of other students, interact with teaching staff and liaise with people in the field. Taking on a social work identity is a social process in that you are gradually becoming incorporated within a professional group. The issues that might arise for you, ('How much do I identify with this group?' or 'How do I assert my independence?'), are similar to those found in other group contexts.

Developing capacity in professional practice is socially situated. That is, capacity and confidence in a particular area (such as social work) grows through engaging with other people and being supported by them in taking on more responsibility. It is the doing of social work with other people that is so important, which is why teaching staff construct group learning experiences. While it might be tempting to groan at the thought of doing yet another role play, these and similar activities play a key part in collaborative practice learning.

One of the benefits of learning with others is the opportunity to receive feedback. There will be opportunities to gain feedback from lecturers and tutors and from your student colleagues, for example through discussing performance in practice simulations. Feedback will also be crucial while on practice placements and will be provided by supervisors, practice teachers, and other professional staff. Another important source of feedback is service users and community members. Increasing emphasis, especially in the UK, is now given to the role of service users in social work education, although there is a lot more to be done to ensure that service users' voices are valued within university settings. Branfield et al. (2007: 13) argue that the purpose of service user feedback 'is to ensure that the new generation of social workers understands the outcomes from social care that people want and the standards of practice they expect.'

Learning with others can be challenging. Conflict can occur, and indeed is likely, around work allocation, being a team player, leadership and commitment. Receiving feedback on your communication skills can feel like a personal attack and different from receiving feedback on more academic work. Here are some strategies to consider.

Feedback strategies

- When asking for feedback ensure you have the time to sit down with the person so that it can be provided in a thoughtful and considered way.
- If appropriate, provide a focus for the feedback – for example, you might tell a service user in advance that you are interested in receiving feedback about how comfortable they were made to feel at the beginning of an interview.
- Don't ask for feedback if you are not in a position to take negative comments on board – in other words, don't ask for it if you only want to hear positive things.
- Be open to hearing positive comments and don't ignore these if also presented with less positive comments.
- Encourage the person providing the feedback to be constructive in their feedback – ask them what they think you could do to improve things.
- If you feel angry or defensive about what is being said, don't react immediately; indicate that you may need some time to process the information.
- If you disagree with something, follow this up with the person at a later date rather than let things stew.

Feedback plays a key role in facilitating reflexivity. This involves not just the feedback received from other people, but also the feedback you can provide to yourself through critical reflection on your own learning. Using feedback positively can help you develop as an emerging social worker.

APPROACHES TO LEARNING AND TEACHING

Most social work programmes incorporate the following aspects:

- foundational learning (e.g. an understanding of sociology, government, human development);
- core learning (e.g. direct practice methods, working within the legal context);
- advanced practice learning (e.g. specialization in work with children and families or mental health);
- supervised practice (i.e. practice placements in the field).

Despite this, considerable diversity still exists in the way programmes are delivered and the learning opportunities that are offered. We now explore some of the different approaches to teaching and learning that you might find in your social work degree.

INSTRUCTIVIST APPROACH

This is the traditional classroom approach to teaching and learning and is typically framed, somewhat pejoratively, as passive learning and as didactic. It involves clearly constructed 'teacher' and 'student' roles where the student is seen as an 'empty vessel' to be filled with the teacher's knowledge and expertise. Acquisition of this knowledge is demonstrated by regurgitating the information, for example during an end-of-semester exam.

While this approach has been substantially critiqued, elements of the instructivist approach can still be found within social work programmes. Lectures are still a common form of content delivery and while interactive approaches have emerged, these can be difficult to manage with large class sizes and in tiered lecture theatres. Moving beyond the instructivist approach can be challenging for both students and staff. Sometimes you may feel a need to be simply 'told how to do it' in a text book fashion. Sometimes teaching staff feel the need to point to important aspects of legislation that they know need to be studied carefully and thoroughly. Nonetheless, in general, the limitations of such an approach are widely recognized and most degrees promote an active learning approach where the focus is on learning through doing.

EXPERIENTIAL LEARNING

Experiential learning, a form of active learning, draws heavily on the work of Kolb (1984) who identified four stages of experiential learning:

- *concrete experience:* where action is being experienced;
- *reflective observation:* where the experience is being reflected upon;
- *abstract conceptualization:* where what was experienced is being made sense of and a model of understanding developed;
- *active experimentation:* where plans for testing the model are put into place.

While any type of experience (e.g. personal experience, practice experience) can be incorporated within this way of learning, much of the literature on experiential learning focuses on how educators can structure meaningful experiences within classroom settings. Typically you are involved in activities such as role plays and games which may be used to simulate practice-type situations. In social work, of course, practice placements provide a unique opportunity for experiential learning.

PROBLEM-BASED LEARNING

Problem-based learning (PBL) is another form of active learning. It involves being engaged with a complex and messy 'real world' hypothetical scenario, in which one or more problems are encountered that need to be overcome. It requires seeking out knowledge as it is relevant to resolving the situation at hand. Typically you would work through a series of stages: defining the problem, gathering information, and constructing a solution. This approach is often used within discrete components of a social work programme (e.g. in tutorials or workshops or as part of an online learning module), but it is also used in some programmes as the primary educational model.

ENQUIRY AND ACTION LEARNING AND ISSUES-BASED LEARNING

Some social work educators and students are concerned that the PBL model reinforces a negative (problem-based) approach to learning that runs counter to anti-oppressive and strengths-based ideas. While most PBL approaches do not advocate it, there may also be a tendency to drift towards a rational and logical approach to 'fixing' the problem. So in social work the PBL approach has been further developed into enquiry and action learning and issues-based learning. For example, the Enquiry and Action Learning model, developed at the University of Bristol, draws heavily on both PBL and reflective learning ideas, and involves 'study units' as the main site for learning. Students work together as groups responding to a specific case scenario (e.g. a family with a child with a disability) over a two week period. The self-directed learning is supported by a range of resources (e.g. written material and access to consultants) and involves a series of reflective learning strategies to help make sense of the learning gained (Taylor, 1996). It is likely that you will be involved in this kind of learning. Here is a typical example of a PBL/issues based approach.

Example of an issues-based learning activity

The following issues-based learning exercise might take place in one class or perhaps over a number of classes, especially if there were assessed tasks linked to the scenario. Learning outcomes include: increased awareness of the emotional dimensions of organizational life and residential settings, increased understanding of other professionals' work roles, and improved capacity to support colleagues in difficult work situations, as well as skills in group work, verbal presentations, and critical thinking. In preparation for the activity, students would read prescribed articles on residential aged care, social work with older people, organizational culture and workplace stress. This could include an article by Grant et al. (2005) which provides a moving account of a student nurse's first experience bathing an older patient.

Scenario

Meadowvale Nursing Home provides residential services to frail older people and people with dementia. It employs a large number of staff, including registered nurses, enrolled nurses, domestic staff, administrative staff, a recreation officer and social worker. While the facility provides therapeutic and recreational activities to residents and day clients, due to resourcing difficulties, most of these activities tend to happen in groups.

You have just finished your first month working at Meadowvale as the part-time social worker. While it is hard to put your finger on it, you feel a little uneasy about the culture of the organization. It's not that it's depressing; in fact it's almost the opposite. Clients are frequently engaged in activities, regular social occasions, and numerous bus trips away, etc. So much emphasis is placed on activities, socializing, and having a good time that you wonder how people manage if they are struggling with personal issues or if they prefer to be alone. You have witnessed people being forced, by the pressure of staff, to join in when

(Continued)

(Continued)

it is clear that they don't want to or are not fully able to. Other times you have seen people sitting off by themselves, apparently uninterested in all the activity going on around them. When people have become tearful or distressed, you have occasionally seen staff ignore them or try to 'jolly them along'. Often staff don't have the time or don't seem to be inclined to just sit with the person to support them. When discussing these situations with colleagues, you get the sense that these people – referred to as 'non-joiners' – are treated as somehow problematic. Many of these people are referred to you as the social worker, which seems to add to their stigmatization.

Activities

1. In a group, discuss what you think is happening in this organization.
2. How are the emotional dimensions of the work with older people being handled? What do you think could be done better?
3. What could you do to challenge the stigmatization of the 'non-joiners' in the organization?
4. What are some of the challenges facing nursing and personal care staff in their work? Consider the account of a student nurse practitioner in the article by Grant et al. (2005).
5. How could you work with staff to support them in managing the emotional dimensions of their work and to improve their practice?
6. At the monthly senior staff meeting, you are asked to present your thoughts about the organization and how the social work service can be developed. In your group, prepare a presentation to the staff meeting that acknowledges some of the issues you have identified. You should draw on appropriate literature and research evidence for your presentation.
7. Deliver your presentation to the class.
8. In your group, discuss key areas of learning from the scenario and feedback key points to the class.

You may face some challenges in problem-based and issues-based learning. Such as:

- Overcoming the need to be 'told how to do it' and becoming an independent learner.
- Seeing academic staff as resources for learning rather than as teachers.
- Feeling comfortable with moving between gathering and applying information and reformulating the problem or issue at hand.
- Being able to analyse relevant information (e.g. research) and seeing the issue holistically.
- Being able to establish goals and work independently and cooperatively within a group.
- Engaging honestly and openly in reflective activities so that you can learn from the experience.

COLLABORATIVE LEARNING

In social work education, you are likely to come across collaborative learning in group project work, such as in the problem-based learning model. This provides a unique way for you to learn about other students' professional and disciplinary backgrounds and develop skills in joint or team working (e.g. Pollard et al., 2004). Increasingly collaborative learning strategies (e.g. via wikis – web pages that can be authored and edited by a group of people) are being used in online learning resources, such as Blackboard and WebCT.

REFLECTIVE LEARNING

As we discussed in Chapter 1, reflective learning is central to reflective practice and emerges through the experience of engaging in action. Reflective learning is an alternative – perhaps even an antidote – to technical, rational, and mechanistic approaches to generating and applying knowledge in practice. It aims to stimulate creative responses to complex situations, rather than rely on programmatic answers. You are likely to be engaged in various reflective learning strategies, such as:

- learning journals and observational reports to record learning experiences;
- reflective components in written assignments;
- debriefing activities and critical incident analysis to facilitate reflection on important events;
- learning partners to share ideas with;
- self-assessment schedules to assist you to define your learning goals and assess your achievements (adapted from Boud and Knights, 1996).

As a reflective learner you would be encouraged to attend to how you feel and respond to experiences; that is, to the emotional content and context. It is also likely that you would be asked think critically about power relations in the construction of knowledge.

LEARNING FOR PRACTICE COMPETENCE

The primary aim of your social work degree is to help you become an effective social work practitioner. Of course different people may have different views about what you as a beginning practitioner should look like: such as how much knowledge you should have of the law; or how skilled you should be in conducting risk assessments; or how able you are to critically analyse the organizations that employ you. In order to establish a benchmark for what should be expected, professional and regulatory bodies in the UK, Australia and elsewhere have set out a series of competences or occupational standards which beginning practitioners are expected to be able to meet and demonstrate. In this section we examine some of the specific learning issues that need to be considered in order to develop, demonstrate, and analyse practice competence.

Social work standards focusing on competences draw attention to social workers' accountability not just to managers, governments, and funders, but also to communities and service users. The National Occupational Standards in the UK, for example, do this while at the same time give prominence to reflective practice and to values and ethics as key aspects of social work education. You can use analysis and demonstration of competence for critical reflection.

PRACTICE LEARNING PLACEMENTS

Having said that the overall purpose of social work education is to prepare you for practice, it is also true that some particular components of a degree are more focused on practice learning than others. Practice placements provide an opportunity for you to work in a human service agency and receive dedicated supervision and practice teaching from an experienced social worker. While you will be accountable to the organization that hosts the placement and must operate in line with their policies and procedures, the main purpose of the placement is to achieve some of your own key learning goals.

Each placement will be different depending on the agency, client group, dominant methods and models of practice, and your own learning priorities. However, there are some common issues to be aware of:

- *The placement matching process.* This is complex and occurs in a context of scarce resources (i.e. the number of placements available). Staff take into account a wide range of factors in matching you with a placement, such as your preferences, prior experience, gaps in learning, availability of transport, and family and other responsibilities.
- *Self presentation.* How you dress, how you communicate in a professional manner, and how you fit in with the expectations of the organization are vital to the success of your social work placement. For example, you would present yourself very differently if you were placed on an elderly care ward in a hospital compared with having a placement in a youth or homeless street based service.
- *Focus on your learning.* It is easy to slip into a worker role, especially if you have spent many years in employment. This is where the relationship between you and your supervisor or practice teacher really comes to the fore in creating the space for processing and extending your learning and professional development.
- *Challenges and support.* Placement can be a challenging time and not everything will go to plan. So it is important for you to think through and set up sources of support. While this might involve your supervisor, it might also involve others, such as fellow students and friends.

Developing a support group with others doing social work is so helpful. In fact, for me it is crucial. (SW student)

Here are some tips for getting the most out of your placements:

Tips for making the most out of practice learning placements

- Seek out feedback from different people (including supervisor, colleagues, and clients).
- Ask questions if unsure.
- Be proactive – don't ignore problems in the hope they will go away.
- Identify yourself as a student practitioner and openly acknowledge your learning role.
- Find someone to act as a mentor.
- Read in a focused way, but don't ignore important sources of information (e.g. agency documents, policy reports, academic literature, research literature).
- Keep a reflective journal.
- Regularly document examples from your practice that demonstrate competence across relevant standards (e.g. in the UK the National Occupational Standards).
- Use different techniques (e.g. process recording, critical incident reporting) to highlight learning from particular experiences.
- Get together with other students in the same agency or nearby to share experiences and gain support.

THE STUDENT-SUPERVISOR/PRACTICE TEACHER RELATIONSHIP

Your placement supervisor undertakes a number of different roles, including:

- *A supportive role:* assisting you to get settled into the placement and providing encouragement when difficulties are encountered.
- *An educative role:* providing instruction and learning opportunities to improve competence and facilitate professional development.
- *A mediating role:* liaising between you and others in the agency (including more senior staff and managers) if difficulties arise or conflict occurs.
- *An administrative role:* ensuring that you are complying with agency and university procedures.
- *An assessing role:* evaluating performance in line with practice standards and competences and providing evidence on this to the university.

Occasionally there can be tension between these different roles and difficulties may arise in the relationship, especially if the roles are not clearly understood by both parties. For example, if the assessing role is not properly acknowledged and the supportive role is overemphasized, it may be difficult for you to accept any con-structively critical comments that the supervisor may make at the mid- or final-evaluation points. It is important for both you and your supervisor to be aware of the boundaries of the relationship and to use power and authority appropriately. It is very helpful to discuss this early on. Supervision contracts are used in some placements as a means of formalizing the relationship so that each knows where they stand.

AREAS OF PRACTICE COMPETENCE

Different areas of practice competence are expected of you as a social worker in the making. As highlighted in Chapter 1, the key roles identified in the UK's National Occupational Standards cover important aspects of practice, such as assessing, plan-ning, carrying out and reviewing work with individuals, families, carers, groups and communities. They also relate to the provision of support and advocacy, risk man-agement, and being able to manage your work and be accountable. Similarly the Australian Association of Social Workers' (2003) practice standards relate to areas such as: direct practice, service management, organizational development and sys-tem change, policy, research, and education and professional development. Once you graduate you will be expected to demonstrate these standards.

In working towards becoming a competent practitioner you might like to consider:

- Your own values, the values of the social work profession and how to draw on these to inform ethical practice, including ethical decision making.
- Your own strengths and limitations and a capacity to engage in education and professional development activities to improve professional ability.
- How to use yourself and your communication skills purposefully when engaging with people in different settings, including with service users, colleagues and supervisors.

- The different sources of knowledge, including how to draw on social work practice theories and research findings when engaging in and evaluating practice.
- How to be effective, ethical, and strategic organisational operators, especially in facilitating and leading organizational change in line with social work values.
- How to work effectively within the legal context, but also how the law can be used to promote the rights and opportunities of service users and community members.
- How to engage in policy practice – that is, initiate, develop, implement and evaluate policy reform.

EVIDENCING PRACTICE COMPETENCE

At various points you will be required to analyse and critique your practice, showing how you meet the standards and demonstrate the competences. This would most likely happen during your mid- and final-placement evaluations, as well as through other activities, such as case study essays, oral presentations, and being observed in practice. In demonstrating competence you will usually need to provide specific examples, such as a narrative about a practice experience, with some conclusions about how the standard was met. As mentioned earlier, this gives you the opportunity to reflect critically on this experience, and what you learnt from it and how you might do things differently next time. You don't always have to present the most positive picture of yourself and your work; it is also important to demonstrate that you can learn from mistakes. An example of writing to evidence practice competence is provided in Chapter 9.

FITNESS TO PRACTISE

Most people would probably agree that not everyone is suited to be a social worker. And while some social work programmes carefully screen candidates prior to admission (including criminal record checks), sometimes there will be people already undertaking the programme who shouldn't qualify as a social worker. In most cases, people come to the realization themselves, or with the assistance of staff, that social work is not for them and often some academic credit can be transferred from the social work degree to another programme. In other situations, students fail key components of the course and, depending on the university's rules, may be blocked from proceeding.

When a student fails a practice placement it can be very difficult for both students and supervisors. However, it is not done lightly and is very important for maintaining the standards of the profession and for enabling students to find a new career path. In some cases a student may be withdrawn from a placement because there is a concern that their behaviour may harm service users or community members. Increasingly universities also have 'fitness to practise' policies which allow them to exclude a student from the programme or refuse to place a student in an agency if they engage in conduct that is unethical, criminal, represents a risk to public safety or is likely to bring the profession into disrepute (among other standards). In all of these cases, it is likely that there would be appeals processes in place and opportunities for the student to seek advice and representation (e.g. from a student union or a lawyer). These processes are vital aspects of ensuring that the community can have trust in the social work profession.

CONCLUSION

This chapter has been about how you, as a social worker in the making, can jump in and make the most of the learning opportunities available. Being an effective social worker means not standing on the sidelines, but getting involved in, and assisting others to negotiate, the issues and politics of everyday life. Being a student social worker is a once-in-a-career opportunity to have a go, try things out, and be supported in your learning.

Finding out more

Websites

The Social Work and Social Policy Subject Centre (SWAP) of the UK's Higher Education Academy provides a wide range of resources aimed to improve social work students' learning experiences.
http://www.swap.ac.uk/

AASWWE is the Australian Association for Social Work and Welfare Education. The website includes free access to their online journal, *Advances in Social Work and Welfare Education*, as well as the journal *Women in Welfare Education*.
http://www.aaswwe.asn.au/

Reading

Cleak, H. and Wilson, J. (2007) *Making the Most of Field Placement*, 2nd edn. South Melbourne: Thomson.

Neugebauer, J. and Evans-Brain, J. (2009) *Making the Most of Your Placement*. London: SAGE.

White, S., Fook, J. and Gardiner, F. (2006) *Critical Reflection in Health and Social Care*. Milton Keynes: Open University Press.

5 ENGAGING WITH RESEARCH: MAKING THE CONNECTIONS

Social workers are expected to draw on research in their practice and even research their own interventions, so social work students need to develop a good understanding of research activities and their relevance for practice. In this chapter we look at:

- different approaches to social work research;
- approaches to data analysis;
- evaluating research literature;
- developing a literature review.

It's just such a good feeling … to pull up a journal … so that, like, you know the research has just been done. (SW student)

When you start to engage with social work research, usually through a subject on research methods, like this student quoted above, the idea of research in your student and later professional career often begins to make sense. But some of you may be surprised to find research subjects in your social work degree, and indeed some of you may feel a bit challenged when confronted with the prospect of studying statistics.

I'm struggling a bit with the research subjects. (SW student)

But as we outlined in Chapter 1, research is increasingly seen as an essential aspect of social work practice. It is a key source of knowledge informing social workers' assessments and interventions. It is used as a basis for developing organizational and social policy. And it is employed to evaluate the effectiveness of the interventions and programmes developed. Without research, social workers would be flying in the dark, with little understanding of the value of their activities, their impact on clients and service users, and their wider benefit to society.

Everyone has some degree of competence in engaging with research. Most of us have been surveyed at one time or another – often by phone just before dinner! – and probably have views on whether or not the survey questions were able to capture our perspective accurately. Most of us would have read and thought critically about research findings reported in the media, such as the results of opinion polls on the preferred prime minister or the findings on the latest medical advance. Social work students bring critical and logical thinking, interviewing and communication skills, and skills in planning and organizing work to research. So while there are areas for growth and development in terms of research capacity and understanding, you already carry experience, knowledge, and skills that can be effectively used in engaging in research.

SOCIAL WORKERS' RESEARCH ROLES

What roles do social workers and you, as social workers in the making, have in relation to research? First, you are frequently consumers of research. That is, you often need to read research – including a study's methodology and findings – and draw out implications for your own work and study. This involves reading and evaluating research articles (such as those published in scholarly journals) and other types of research reports, in addition to making sense of research presentations at conferences and seminars. Practitioners and students need to be able to weigh up the strengths and limitations of the research reported and consider carefully what can or cannot be applied to their own practice.

Second, social workers also often engage in their own research which is designed to create new knowledge. A common form of social work research, as we discuss shortly, is developing and implementing a survey or focus group to help understand how clients experience a service. So social workers also need skills in setting up and carrying out research projects. This would involve identifying the problem to be addressed, developing research questions, establishing and implementing a methodology, analysing the findings, and identifying the implications of the study.

Third, social workers and students are often involved as partners or participants in research activities. Given their organizational positions, many practitioners are involved in facilitating access to a research sample (e.g. by promoting a research project to clients or community members). They may be involved in making decisions about whether or not research projects should proceed or whether or not the organization should support them. For example, a social worker might be involved in reviewing the way in which participant consent is obtained before referring on clients to be interviewed by a researcher. They may also be themselves the subjects or participants of research projects, such as in a study that surveys social workers' experience of workplace stress. In each of these roles, the social worker needs to be able to evaluate the quality of the research proposed in order to make a decision about authorizing the research or being a participant.

I guess research can be defined on many levels but we all probably do a type of research on a daily basis. I must say doing this paper [in a research course] has made me think a bit more when planning something at work, wondering what the end result will be, very thought provoking (SW student, cited in Gibbs and Stirling, 2010: 7)

In the early stages of your social work degree it is unlikely that you would be initiating your own research project or be a partner in research activities. What you certainly would be called on to do, though, is to read research articles and research reports and to be able to make sense of these. So in this chapter our focus is mainly on reading research for social work. There are a number of valuable texts covering the other aspects of research practice and we highlight some of these at the end of the chapter.

One aspect of studying research methods that is sometimes off-putting is its terminology. So we introduce you to some key terms and concepts below.

APPROACHES TO RESEARCH IN SOCIAL WORK

QUALITATIVE AND QUANTITATIVE APPROACHES

We start with some of the different approaches to research in social work. The first key distinction to make is the often talked about differences between qualitative and quantitative research.

While many researchers critique the splitting of research thinking into qualitative and quantitative, Bryman (2004) argues that it is a useful contrast to make. Broadly, qualitative research relates to research processes that try to understand a phenomenon within the complexity of its wider context. For example, in studying women who have been victims of domestic violence, a qualitative approach might explore in detail individual women's experiences within the context of their own life situation, history, community and family. From this, arises a contextualised, in-depth and nuanced understanding of what it is like to be a victim of domestic violence.

Whereas a qualitative approach develops a broad and detailed understanding of the issue under examination, a quantitative approach is more about clearly defining the nature of the issue and then measuring the extent to which it appears within a particular population. Quantitative research is often also concerned with delineating cause and effect links. For example, in relation to women victims of domestic violence, a quantitative approach might involve developing (or using an existing) instrument that identifies domestic violence and then using that to measure the extent of such violence in a particular group of women, such as older women. The research could also include measures of other phenomena, such as degree of social isolation, to see if they are related to, and possibly a cause of, what is being studied. In this case, it might be hypothesized that domestic violence is more common in socially isolated older women than those who have active social networks, because their violent partners are not as subjected to the controlling influences of friends and family members. All this would require a high degree of clarity in defining and measuring domestic violence and social isolation.

There can be a range of factors influencing a researcher's decision to employ either a qualitative or a quantitative approach. For many, the main priority is the type of research question that is being asked. If, for example, the research question is about people's unique experiences then a qualitative approach might be selected. If it is about how one factor affects another, a quantitative approach may be chosen. This can relate to the type of knowledge or theory that is being developed. Qualitative approaches tend to be most useful in developing new theory – starting from the bottom up, for example by exploring people's experiences and then developing theoretical ideas from this information. This is often referred to as an inductive or theory building approach. Quantitative approaches are often used to test theory; a deductive approach. This involves examining (measuring) the extent to which already developed theoretical ideas are found to be true in different population groups.

For other researchers, the decision to use qualitative or quantitative approaches is made on the basis of a political or philosophical stance in relation to the nature of the world and how best to understand it. Some researchers – referred to as positivists – tend to believe that the best way to generate knowledge is to measure it through scientific means. These researchers usually prefer quantitative over qualitative methods. Interpretivist researchers, on the other hand, believe that reality is complex and highly subjective – that one person's reality is different from another's – and that this is best understood through in-depth qualitative investigations. Positivist research strives for objectivity and neutrality on the part of the researcher. In contrast, interpretivist research sees the researcher as a co-constructor of meaning with research participants and thus cannot be treated as a neutral party. Another group, critical researchers who are concerned to expose and address social inequalities, will often employ both qualitative and quantitative approaches for different purposes. Quantitative approaches may be used to expose the nature and extent of disadvantage experienced by a population group such as refugees. Qualitative approaches may be employed to enable this marginalized group to tell their unique stories and to have their voice heard.

It is worth noting that the debates that can be seen between proponents of quantitative and qualitative methods often arise from these different world views and different perspectives on how knowledge should be generated. For social workers, however, it is usually the case that they develop and use both qualitative and quantitative research, with both being equally valued depending on the nature of the research issue. So many research projects will involve both quantitative and qualitative components in a way that generates a much fuller understanding of the issue than if only one approach was used.

Wow, until beginning this paper [in a research course] I was quite daunted by the word RESEARCH but now can see that it can be a part of everyday life. (SW student, cited in Gibbs and Stirling, 2010: 7)

EXPERIMENTS AND OUTCOME STUDIES

However, almost contradicting the previous point, experiments and outcome studies especially value quantitative methods as a means of establishing cause and effect links. Many researchers believe that the best way of establishing such links is by striving to achieve the rigorous standards set in the 'classic experiment'. This approach to research, which is rare in social work but common in medicine and psychology, involves the studying (usually by observation) of phenomena under laboratory conditions. It typically involves the active manipulation of an independent variable, that is the one that causes an effect, to see what impact it has on a dependent variable, that is the one that is affected. For example, if a psychologist was testing the effect of exposure to violent video games on aggressive impulses, they might expose a research participant to a violent video game (the independent variable) and then test the participant's tendency to prefer aggressive strategies (the dependent variable) over non-aggressive when presented with a case example involving family conflict.

In addition to being carried out under laboratory conditions, the classic experiment usually has three other key features: a pre-test and post-test, control and experimental groups, and randomized allocation to these groups. Pre- and post-test refers to the testing of the dependent variable before and after the independent variable is introduced. In the prior example, the research participants' aggressive impulses would be measured before (pre-test) and after (post-test) the video game (the independent variable) was played. This helps to see how much influence the independent variable has on the dependent variable. To improve the rigour of the experiment even more, the study can be split into two groups. Those people who are allocated to the experimental group, also known as the intervention or treatment group, are exposed to the independent variable, that is, they play the video game. Those who are in the control group are not exposed to the independent variable, that is, they don't play the game. If the aggressive impulses of the control group at post-test are the same as they were at pre-test but the experimental group's impulses have increased, then this helps clarify that this was a product of playing the game, and not due to other external factors. Randomized allocation of research participants to either the control or experimental group, for example, by picking names out of a hat, further enhances the rigour of the research.

Social workers are most likely to encounter aspects of the experimental design when exposed to outcome studies. Outcome studies aim to evaluate the effects of implementing a particular programme, treatment or intervention with a particular group of people. In these studies, the outcome that is desired is the dependent variable, while the programme, treatment or intervention is the independent variable. Say a social worker developed a programme to support young parents to help reduce their social isolation. In this case the independent variable would be the support programme, and the dependent variable would be the degree of isolation experienced.

Experiments and outcome studies are especially significant in discussions about evidence-based practice because these approaches are sometimes highlighted as producing the best quality evidence on which to base practice decisions. While most social work research will not be able to achieve the standards of scientific rigour set by the classic lab-controlled experiment, it is sometimes, unfairly, critiqued on this basis. Nonetheless outcome studies, given an understanding of their limitations, are a valuable means of evaluating how social work interventions make a difference in people's lives.

> I have learned that research has a significant role in improving the effectiveness of social work practice; that research can contribute to wider policy change. (SW student, cited in Gibbs and Stirling, 2010: 7)

SURVEYS

Like experiments and outcome studies, surveys best lend themselves to a quantitative approach, although they will often have a qualitative component. Surveys study what is 'naturally' occurring within particular social settings or for a particular group of people. They often adopt a 'cross-sectional' design in that they aim to study a good cross-section of the population under investigation. This is achieved by sampling a group from the population, the aim of which is usually to achieve a probability sample. This is a sample where every member of the population has an equal chance, that is, a probability, of being selected (e.g. by a random sampling technique). This helps increase the chance that findings relating to the sample can be generalized to the wider population. For example, if you were studying prisoners' motivation to undertake further education a random sample might involve randomly selecting a group of 500 prisoners from the total national prisoner population. You can see that this might be a more representative sample than if you only studied prisoners from one particular correctional facility (which may or may not have educational initiatives in place).

Unlike experiments and outcome studies, surveys usually do not involve the direct manipulation of the independent variable. Rather, the sample is divided up into different groups according to one or more independent variables to see if there are any differences between the groups. In the prisoner study, we might want to see if motivation to undertake further education is related to gender. In this case the dependent variable would be educational motivation and the independent variable would be gender. The sample would then be split according to gender to see if educational motivation was higher or lower for women compared to men.

Surveys are usually delivered by a questionnaire in paper form or via the internet. Sometimes they are delivered by way of a structured interview, either face-to-face or by telephone. Typically you are asked a series of closed questions that give a limited range of responses from which you can choose. These questions produce quantitative data aimed at measuring the specific phenomena under investigation. For example, prisoners' educational motivation might be measured by questions that include information about their views on how useful they think education is, the number of times they have enrolled in a course, and their desire to learn. Qualitative data can be generated by open-ended questions that ask the respondent to write down their thoughts or talk at more length about an issue or experience.

Surveys are very common in social work research. Many practitioners would at some point be involved in surveying client satisfaction and most would be routinely accessing survey findings to inform their work.

QUALITATIVE INTERVIEWS

Qualitative interviews, also referred to as in-depth interviews, are the most common way of generating detailed qualitative data. As with survey interviews, they can be delivered by telephone, although they are probably best done face-to-face. This is because the interviewer plays a key role in making the interviewee feel comfortable so that they might be prepared to share their story, which could include very personal information. For example, in a research study looking at the experiences of bereaved parents, the interviewees might need to feel supported before they are able to disclose the emotional impact the experience has had on them. Usually the interviews are audio-recorded and then transcribed into a written document, which is subsequently analysed.

Qualitative interviews vary in structure and standardization. Unstructured interviews are those that have a number of broad areas for discussion (often listed as topic areas in an interview guide) and as the interview unfolds the interviewee raises issues that are important to them. Semi-structured interviews will usually have some specifically formulated questions (in an interview schedule), as well as varying degrees of opportunity for providing more detail and raising other issues. Standardization refers to the number of questions/topics that are raised with every interviewee. It is likely that in unstructured interviews there is a low degree of standardization as the direction the interview takes determines what questions are followed up with each individual. It is also common for qualitative interviews to have a small quantitative component in order to make sure some basic information, such as demographic information, is collected for every participant.

Social workers bring many skills to qualitative interviewing, not least their ability to form appropriate professional relationships and facilitate personal disclosure. It is important for students and practitioners to remember, though, that a research interview is different from a social work interview, in that the purpose of a research interview is the collection of data for research purposes. If emotional support, counselling, or another type of social work intervention is required then this is usually provided by a qualified person at the end of the interview or the interviewee is referred to services that can provide this assistance.

FOCUS GROUPS

Focus groups are group-based interviews, usually five to 12 people, led by a facilitator 'focusing' on a specific topic. They are used in a wide range of contexts, including in market and political research, and are increasingly valued as a method of social work research (Cohen and Garrett, 1999). Focus groups may generate different types of data from individual interviews in that they can capitalize on group processes – such as the creativity that emerges from a group brainstorming session. The members of focus groups are often specifically selected for their experience or expertise in relation to the issue discussed. They can be particularly useful for investigating issues of concern for hard-to-reach or marginalized groups. For example, young drug users may feel more comfortable talking about their issues within a focus group involving their peers than if they were interviewed one-on-one. Another key benefit of focus groups, especially for social work researchers, is that useful data can not only be generated from the content of the group (i.e. what people say), but also by observing the group members' behaviour. They may be audio recorded or, to better analyse the group processes, video recorded.

Now that we have discussed briefly the main concepts, terms and approaches relevant to research in social work, it may be useful for you to activate some of this information.

Activity

1. Identify a research topic of interest and that is appropriate to discuss with your classmates. Write down a couple of research questions.
2. What would be the advantages and disadvantages of a survey questionnaire compared with an unstructured qualitative interview to investigate this topic?
3. Prepare a short questionnaire (for the survey) and a broad interview guide (for the qualitative interview).
4. Trial your questionnaire and interview guide with some of your classmates. Jot down their responses to your questions.
5. How did the information collected by the survey questionnaire differ from that collected by the unstructured interview?
6. Which type of interview seemed best suited to the research topic?

APPROACHES TO DATA ANALYSIS

When you read a research article you need to understand what form of data analysis has been used to understand and interpret the information gathered and its appropriateness and validity for the type of project. But analysis is not just used and referred to in academic articles; you also come across it commonly in news reports, documentaries, and investigative journalism where for example, statistics are quoted (indicating quantitative analysis has been used) or conclusions from analysis of case examples are given (indicating qualitative analysis has probably been used). What you don't necessarily know, of course, is whether the analysis was undertaken in an appropriate way. So we will now look at the nature and types of analyses you are likely to encounter or be required to undertake.

QUANTITATIVE DATA ANALYSIS

Basic quantitative analysis is used by most social work researchers. Even those involved in a primarily qualitative study may want to know what percentage of their sample is male or female, younger or older, and so on. Most quantitative studies draw on a range of statistical tests to inform their analysis. While this can seem daunting, the reality for most researchers is that they seek advice from specialists and key texts as they plan their research. Most would also use statistical analysis software, such as SPSS, which is becoming increasingly user-friendly.

In quantitative research, data analysis relies on well designed instruments and questionnaires. A poorly designed scale – for example, one where it is difficult for a respondent to select an appropriate answer – will produce poor data, which will limit the analysis that is possible. Take the following example. A researcher measuring 'age' asked respondents to tick one of the following: 15 and under; 15 to 20; 20 to 25; 25 to 30; 30 to 35; 35 to 40; 40 to 45; 45 to 50; 50 and over. In the first instance this scale is flawed because it is unclear which category people who are aged 15, 20, 25, 30 etc should select. Instead, the categories should be 15 and under; 16 to 20; 21 to 25, etc. Second, it is possible that the group 50 and over is too broad and will contain a much larger number of people than in each of the prior categories. In such a study it would not be possible to distinguish between people who were aged 81 and those aged 51. Perhaps a better way of going about it would be to ask people their age or date of birth and then to categorize into groups later if necessary. So the capacity of quantitative data analysis very much relies on the overall design of the research.

Descriptive statistics, those that describe the data, are a key part of quantitative data analysis. Percentages are a common way of describing the characteristics of a single variable. For example, if a researcher was studying 382 social workers and categorized them into fields of practice (e.g. mental health, children and families) then a percentage would give information about what proportion of the whole sample was in each group. If there were 110 workers in 'children and families', then they represent 28.8 per cent of 382.

Measures of central tendency provide useful summary information. For example, the mean, commonly referred to as the average, of the social worker sample would be calculated by adding up every person's age and then dividing it by the total number of people (i.e. by 382). Association and correlation statistics provide information about the relationships between two or more variables. For example, a statistical test can be used to see if younger or older social workers have different levels of job satisfaction using a satisfaction scale.

The type of statistical test that can be carried out varies according to a number of factors, including the nature of the variables being used, for example if they are numerical and continuous. It may also be possible to carry out tests to estimate the chance, referred to as probability, that the result from a sample will hold true for the population from which it was taken. This type of analysis involves the use of inferential statistics. Checking a research text book will provide more information and can give you guidelines on what test researchers should be using.

QUALITATIVE DATA ANALYSIS

While it is common for people to think about quantitative analysis as being rigorous, in recent years qualitative approaches to data analysis have also become more sophisticated. In part this has been due to the development of qualitative data analysis software, such as NVivo, but it is also due to the concerns of qualitative researchers to maximize quality and replicability. Inevitably, the inductive nature of much qualitative research makes data analysis complex. Imagine a researcher has interviewed 30 people for one hour each. These 30 recorded hours may take up to 150 hours to transcribe and may produce something like 600 pages of transcript. From these pages, the researcher needs to read and re-read, draw out common ideas, code these ideas, check the material again, link different ideas together, and produce a manageable number of themes which summarize all the material.

A range of different approaches has been developed to guide qualitative data analysis. The most common is thematic analysis. This involves multiple stages of coding, whereby the material is read and summarizing words or statements are allocated to different parts of the text. Links are then made to different codes. Some may be similar and grouped together; others might be recoded, and still others might be identified as a sub-category of a larger code. From this coding, broader themes can be developed which summarize the data. In reporting the results, the researcher might explain a theme and then give some examples through direct quotations from the data.

Another approach to analysing qualitative data, that is a specific approach to qualitative research is the grounded theory approach (Glaser and Strauss, 1967; Strauss and Corbin, 1998). While this approach has evolved in different directions in recent years, it was originally conceived as a way of generating theory from data and ensuring that the theory and the researcher remained closely tied (or grounded) to the data. The approach commonly starts with one case, usually one interview, from which particular ideas related to the topic emerge. This then informs who is next selected into the study, and the process continues. Data analysis thus occurs alongside data collection and involves the development of a series of concepts and categories through coding. The processes of coding and further data collection go through a number of stages before more formal theory is developed.

There is a range of other strategies used in qualitative data analysis. Interpretivist researchers often use reflective journals to facilitate an awareness of their impact on the research process. Critical case analysis involves a detailed examination of the data to identify cases running counter to the key themes that have been developed. This ensures that conclusions about themes are not generalized inappropriately to the whole sample.

In thinking about what we have covered so far regarding the nature and style of research you will encounter, you might like to engage in this activity.

Activity

In a group of students discuss and jot down your responses to the following questions:

1. What is one skill that you have that would be useful if you were a social work researcher?
2. How important do you think it is for social workers to know how to conduct research? Indicate the degree of importance from 1 to 10, with 1 equaling 'not important' and 10 equaling 'essential'.

What type of data does each question produce? How could you analyse the answers to each question so that you could provide an accurate and concise summary of your group's responses?

MAKING SENSE OF RESEARCH ARTICLES AND REPORTS

At first glance a research article or report can appear bamboozling. The detail provided in the methodology and findings sections can be quite intimidating for many students. It may be tempting to skip over those sections and jump straight to the discussion and conclusions. However, it is essential that those sections are digested in order to get to grips with what the research is about and, just as importantly, to be able to critically evaluate it and draw conclusions for your own work. The common structure for a research article in a peer-reviewed journal (discussed in Chapter 3) is outlined below.

Common structure of a research article

- Abstract: a brief summary of the purpose, methods, findings and conclusions of the research.
- Key words: four or five words or phrases that indicate what the research is about.
- Introduction or background: setting the scene of the project.
- Literature review: critical evaluation of the research and theoretical literature as related to the topic, identifying gaps or problems, and thus demonstrating the need for the research. May be under different headings or incorporated into the introduction.
- Methods or methodology: an outline of the approach undertaken, including methods of sampling, data collection, data analysis, strategies to maximize the rigorousness of the research, and ethical issues involved in the project.
- Findings or results: a detailed account of the results of the project. May include quotes to illustrate qualitative data and statistical findings to demonstrate quantitative results. May also include comments on the limitations of the project.
- Discussion: a reflection on the nature and significance of the findings in relation to the key research problem or question and in relation to prior research and theorizing.
- Conclusion: a summing up of the key findings and significance of the project.
- References: a list of references cited in the paper.

Many journals have a specific format to which they require researchers to conform. Research reports (as discussed further in Chapter 8) may have less detail on the methodology, which may be located in the introduction section, and will usually have an executive summary, as well as a series of appendices.

So, how can one make sense of the methodology and findings sections? The key question that often needs to be asked is:

- Was the method used appropriate for answering this particular research question or addressing this specific topic?

For example, a research question that focuses on parents' experience raising a child with a disability may be best answered by a qualitative interview rather than a quantitative survey. A project that seeks to measure the impact of new therapeutic treatment for depression may be best conducted via an outcome study rather than a focus group. So, have a look at what the study is addressing and determine if you think the researchers used the best means possible to answer the question. And, importantly, did you get a sense that they were they able to satisfactorily answer the question by the end of the paper?

Another key area for evaluation is whether or not the methodological approach selected was implemented properly or as well as possible, given the conditions under which the research was carried out. For example, did an outcome study have a pre- and post-test of the dependent variable? Did a survey use a probability sample? Was an unstructured qualitative interview flexible enough to allow people to tell their own stories? Inevitably there will be occasions when ideal research standards can't be maintained. It may be unethical to have a control group for an outcome study because these people will be deprived of a potentially valuable treatment or intervention. Or in cases of limited resources, it may be impossible to generate a random sample for a survey. In these cases it is important to see if the researchers acknowledge openly these limitations and make sure that they do not over-reach themselves when making claims about the significance of the findings. If a researcher surveyed members of a public sector union, for example, and was only able to sample members from three branches of the union, then it is important that they do not claim that the results can be generalised to all union members.

For both quantitative and qualitative research there are some techniques that should be used by researchers to maximise the rigorousness or quality of the research. As a research consumer you should be looking to see if any of these were adopted and reported on in the paper. In quantitative research these often include strategies to improve validity and reliability. Validity refers to accuracy of the research, that is, that the findings are actually reporting what they should be reporting. Reliability relates to the consistency of the research, that is, that the questions or instruments are collecting the same kind of information each time they are employed. For qualitative research a degree of trustworthiness in the data is often looked for. This can relate to how believable the findings are, whether they can be transferred to other contexts, if they apply at other times and if they haven't been unduly influenced by the researcher. Strategies to increase trustworthiness can include member checking, where interviewees are provided with a summary of the findings from their interview to see if it accurately reflects their views. Another strategy is peer checking where a researcher's colleague or supervisor analyses a portion of the interview transcripts to see if they produce the same kind of codes and themes as the researcher. Introductory social research texts usually contain a lot of information about these kinds of strategies, for both qualitative and quantitative research, and it may be useful to refer to these when evaluating research articles and reports.

In looking at the findings section of a research paper, what is important is to make sure that there is evidence for the claims being made. Papers reporting qualitative research will usually include summaries of the major themes that emerged with relevant quotes to illustrate these findings. You should be looking to see if the quotes actually do reflect the finding that is being reported. In quantitative papers you will need to be able to read and understand a table or graph and make sure that these tally with what is reported in the text. As mentioned earlier, some key statistics will need to be understood. The key concern is whether there is sufficient evidence for the conclusions made.

I have … learned that it is important to read research critically and not simply accept its findings. (SW student, cited in Gibbs and Stirling, 2010: 7)

There are lots of other questions that can be used to evaluate and critique social work research. Have a look at some examples below.

Questions to guide analysis of research articles

- What new knowledge did the research generate?
- What gaps in the literature did it address?
- Were research participants at risk of harm through involvement?
- Did they receive any benefit?
- Did the research serve any wider social good?
- What are the implications of the research for future policy and practice?

For all of these areas of critique, it is important to recognize that every research project has its limitations. Rarely do researchers have the resources to conduct a project exactly in line with text book standards. So, in evaluating research articles and reports, bear in mind the factors impacting on the research, and weigh these up with the benefits of the study, when drawing implications for your own work.

LITERATURE REVIEWS

As noted, a common feature of research articles and reports is the literature review. A literature review is something you might be required to produce, in order to demonstrate your understanding of a body of research.

Although summarizing key points from the literature is part of the process, a literature review is not a mere descriptive exercise. Literature reviews involve a critical appraisal of the strengths and weaknesses of prior research and theory. The critique should be based on commonly accepted principles in research practice in that area. For example, qualitative research drawing on a grounded theory approach should be critiqued according to the principles of grounded theory methodology, rather than, say, the principles of quantitative methodologies.

There are some different purposes in providing a literature review in a research document:

- demonstrating understanding and mastery of the field;
- identifying gaps and problems in literature: especially in research and theory development;
- providing evidence of the need for a particular study (in terms of both topic and methodology);
- guiding the development and later the presentation of research questions and/or hypotheses.

As a student preparing a literature review, it is inevitable that you will be limited by time and resources. Often it's better to read and review a smaller number of well selected papers than provide a more superficial review of a larger number of papers. Deciding what papers to select will depend on a number of factors:

- reputation of the authors;
- quality of the publication source;
- relevance to research topic;
- quality of the methodology;
- importance in the field;
- date of publication.

As discussed in Chapter 3, different strategies can be employed: searching electronic databases for journal articles, using books from the library, tracking down papers from a reference list, chasing up prior works from key authors, looking at published literature reviews of the field. Although you want your review to be up-to-date, don't forget older seminal works.

There are different ways of structuring a literature review and your decision about how to proceed may vary according to the nature of the overall document and its audience. You could review key works in a chronological order, although this may feel a bit descriptive as you move from one study to the next. Probably a better idea is to structure according to themes so that you can summarize important issues in the literature and refer to multiple studies/works. Sometimes a literature review will start off very broadly by reviewing a large body of literature, and progressively narrow down until it reaches the specific topic of the research. In a general sense, though, every literature review provides a frame for the research: it helps establish the focus and parameters of the study.

When writing a literature review, pay attention to your audience. Make sure you explain what you are doing and why you have chosen to do certain things and not others (e.g. you may have chosen to critique the methodologies of certain studies in more depth because they provide a foundation for your research). You should explain how the review is structured and help them follow your arguments by using headings, links, and summaries. Further advice on how to present academic arguments that are relevant for literature reviews can be found in Chapter 7.

CONCLUSION

Research plays an important part in social work and thus it is a key area of learning for social work students. Studying for social work involves accessing the latest research articles, as well as being able to understand and critically analyse them. You don't need to be an expert statistician to see if the method used was appropriate for the research question or topic, or if the findings of the study have possible implications for policy or practice. What is important, though, is that you don't take an uncritical approach to reading research. All research is limited to some extent and you need to evaluate research reports to see if you can trust their findings. Strategies for critical thinking and reading are examined in more depth in the next chapter.

Finding out more

Websites

The University of York houses the Social Policy Research Unit (SPRU) which conducts social policy research, especially that impacting on health and social care, poverty, welfare, and social work. A range of relevant publications can be accessed from their site.
http://www.york.ac.uk/inst/spru/

A range of resources, including some on evidence-informed practice and knowledge management, can be found at the Scottish Institute for Research and Innovation in the Social Services.
http://www.iriss.org.uk

The research website of the National Association of Social Workers in the United States contains detailed information about social work research in a wide range of areas: from adoption to violence and injury.
http://www.naswdc.org/research/Default.asp

The Society for Social Work Research, based in the United States, is an international organization aiming to increase networks among social work researchers and to help social workers become more involved in research activities.
http://www.sswr.org/

Reading

Alston, M. and Bowles, W. (2003) *Research for Social Workers: An Introduction*, 2nd edn. St Leonards: Allen & Unwin.

Bryman, A. (2004) *Social Research Methods*, 3rd edn. Oxford: Oxford University Press.

Neuman, W.L. (2010) *Social Research Methods: Qualitative and Quantitative Approaches*, 7th edn. Boston: Allyn & Bacon.

In addition to being an essential guide to a variety of qualitative and quantitative methods, Neuman provides a good overview of literature reviews, which includes examples of a good and bad review.

6

CRITICAL THINKING, READING AND WRITING: GETTING THE BRAIN INTO GEAR

In this chapter we look at critical thinking generally, what it involves and how to develop the necessary skills. We examine annotated extracts from articles and books, as well as critical reviews. You will learn how to:

- read critically;
- demonstrate critical thinking, and engage with other writers;
- structure a critical review.

I was thinking, 'Oh my goodness, am I the only person who doesn't have a clue what half those words were she just said?' (SW student)

I really didn't understand what 'critically analyse' meant before. (SW student)

WHAT IS CRITICAL THINKING IN SOCIAL WORK?

Rather than provide a list of the processes of critical thinking, we consider the views of a small group of social work lecturers who discussed critical thinking in the context of studying for social work. An edited version of the recorded discussion appears below. The discussion focused on critical thinking in the context of social work and social development, and on its importance in academic work in the discipline.

What do you understand critical thinking to be in the context of social work and social development?

Lecturer 1

Well, I can start off by saying that I think, in the social realms, critical thinking implies that you do not take things at face value, that you look underneath the information to see where it has come from, who's said it, what it purports to be about, and what it might really be about.

(Continued)

(Continued)

Lecturer 4

I think in social work and in social development it's also a strong link to practice so it's about applying the theoretical tools to practice situations and using them effectively.

Lecturer 3

I was always taught that the assumptions that we put forward are very important as they play themselves out in the way people speak, or how we define things. It's important to make assumptions and values explicit particularly in social research.

It's important then to be able to do reflective practice, or somehow link theory and practice together, which I think is perhaps quite unique, in an applied sense, to social work, social development, areas where people get their hands dirty. So critical thinking, on the ground, requires you to think very carefully about pre-suppositions, about assumptions and about definitions.

Lecturer 1

That all flows into talking about policy, and critical thinking about policy, because what can you set it up against? You can set it up against description. You can describe a policy, you can describe the background, you can outline what the policy says and what it says it's supposed to do. But critical thinking will pull that apart, will tease out not only what it says it's doing, but what it is actually doing. So that relates to everyone's comments about work on the ground. What is actually happening, how is it affecting real people? And at a theoretical level what are the tools one can bring to understanding that? One could look at equity and rights and social justice as being critical tools to use to look at a policy, or a log frame, or an action happening in a community work setting, or in research. There are others, of course, but you bring those critical tools, theoretical tools, to bear on what's going on.

Lecturer 3

I think another important component is that you need to be selective, you have to be aware of the sorts of tools that you can bring, and how you apply them in different ways. There's an awful lot of information available and so students have to be very selective and being selective is a critical skill in itself. The other part of that is how they then give *meaning* to what that selected information is about, because critical thinking is not about delivering up a set of pat answers to something – of course not. I think that's the critical work, being both selective, but also looking at how meaning occurs.

Lecturer 2

To me critical thinking is [asking]: Who says it? What's their position? What's informing their thought, etc.? What are the implications?

How do you expect your students to demonstrate critical thinking?

Lecturer 3

Often a student responds to a text with description. You know, repeating it in paraphrased fashion. Although I've said clearly from the beginning of session 'If you want to achieve a higher mark, then you need to bring in the different theoretical perspectives'.

You bring in different theoretical orientations to sharpen perspectives. It seems to me that where critical thinking works best, and where I can see it operating, is when a student can do both the practical reality as well as the theoretical understanding of that practical reality. So to me, that reflects the critical process.

(Continued)

(Continued)

Lecturer 3

We're asking them to be active rather than passive, to be engaged with others around them. They'll often score better, of course, when they demonstrate that.

What kind of comments about critical thinking do you find yourself writing to students?

Lecturer 1

The most common thing I would be writing is 'this is just description', reflecting the fact that the person has not thought critically about what they've discovered. ... because, they have not engaged in a critical manner with the content they have discovered. So they haven't asked whether it's doing what it should be doing. They haven't put it up against some of those frameworks that we require about critical thinking.

Lecturer 2

The question is very often, is it true? This is to test information ... against reality.

Lecturer 1

Yes that's right. So, in various cases, I think that would be the most fundamental one.

Lecturer 4

Sometimes students make fairly wild assertions without providing substantial justification and that's often a problem.

Lecturer 3

Yes, one of the worst problems is that they don't give any examples. They don't actually engage with any material; instead they write really high falutin', general, abstract, generalized, wild assertions with no examples and/or no evidence to back up their case.

Lecturer 1

I think everyone has said something that I think is so important in any social setting, or social work or community work, social development, regarding critical thinking, and that is that you cannot work to a formula. And that is why critical thinking is so important: that you have to be able to think something through in a critical manner in its context and as it applies in a particular situation.

(The Learning Centre, UNSW, 2009: 13–15)

WHAT IS CRITICAL THINKING THEN? SUMMING UP

As you can see, critical thinking involves a range of different activities. The key components are: asking questions, reflecting, evaluating, and, in a social work context, applying to social and individual situations.

At university a lot of critical thinking is in relation to reading and discussing texts (here we mean any piece of academic writing, not just textbooks). Critical thinking involves a range of mental processes but, in an academic context, basically it involves engaging with the text, asking questions of it, and making some kind of evaluation. It is not – or should not be – carping negative criticism. Rather than thinking in terms of criticizing someone's work – which many students often feel uncomfortable about – it can be freeing to think in terms of having a conversation with someone about a topic of mutual interest. Kamler and Thomson (2006), following Smyth, suggest that students writing a literature review think of working with the literature (that is, the body of scholarly writings on a subject) as a dinner party. This can be a useful analogy for thinking about any kind of work with other people's writing on a topic. The student invites the guests and cooks the dinner, lets the writers talk about their work, and importantly, '*uses* what they have said, rather than just being grateful that they have come' (p.38) (authors' italics). While you might not want to have a dinner party, the idea of a conversation can be empowering and allow you to relate a text to your own purposes in writing. It also makes it easier to be constructive in your comments, rather than simply negative. When commenting on a text, it's important to respect other people's work, and focus on the ideas or information if offers, rather than the omissions or inadequacies.

WHAT QUESTIONS TO ASK?

I just say read, just read and try to understand. Eventually, eventually, it all comes together. (SW student)

First, be curious about the text.

- What's it about?
- What type of text is it?
- Is it a research report, a policy document, a theoretical article, or a practice text?
- Who wrote it?
- What do you know about the author?
- Who is the publisher? Is it a reputable publisher in your area? When was it first published?

And, importantly,

- What are you asking of the text?
- What are you looking for in the text?

Get a general idea of a book's content:

- look at the table of contents;
- read the blurb on the back cover;
- skim through the book reading the general introduction;

and then

- read the introduction to each chapter.

Look at the structure of the book, how it's organized. Scan for particular topics that are relevant to your assignment. Decide whether you are going to read all of it or a couple of chapters. For a journal article, read the summary or abstract and think about if, and how, it's relevant for your purposes.

Then read more slowly, looking, in particular, at the introduction ₍
where the writer states their aim or purpose in writing, and their pos₍
ment on an issue. It's useful to get into the habit of marking these points
ticular symbol (star, circle, whatever you want) as this helps you to becom
the writer's intentions, and their particular stance on a topic and their devₑ
of it through their writing. It also helps you to find the significant points
when you start writing.

Consider the following examples:

1. (from the introduction)

Evidence-based practice (EBP) is having a major impact in medicine, nursing, and other health care
professions, both in the United States and internationally. ... Within social work EBP is influential in some ← **Overview**
English-speaking countries, such as the UK and Australia. ...

Some recent publications describe its possibilities (Gambrill, 1999, 2001), advocate for standards (Rosen
and Proctor, 2002), and suggest cautions (Witkin and Harrison, 2001). Though helpful, these articles do ← Useful sum-
not place EBP within its contexts. In addition, these authors do not draw lessons from the experience of | mary of other
other professions with EBP. [purpose and scope] The purpose of this article is to present such an analysis | works on the
and learn from the experiences of others. I based my analysis primarily on evidence-based medicine | same topic,
(EBM), the parent discipline of EBP, but I also draw on evidence-based nursing and evidence-based social | what they do,
work in the United Kingdom. | and don't do.

From my analysis and reflections on the nature of social work practice, I *conclude* that EBP in social
work rests on four cornerstones: (1) research and theory; (2) practice wisdom, or what Willie and other ← Writer's argu-
professionals have learned from our clients, which also includes professional values; (3) the person of | ment; notice
the practitioner, or our personal assumptions, values, biases, and world views; and (4) what clients bring | italicized verbs.
to practice situations. In addition, based on my readings on the philosophy of science, I *view* evidence
from any source as provisional, meaning understandings are open to modification as new evidence
unfolds (Popper, 1969; Shaw and Shaw, 1997). Finally, I *show* that falsification – that is, a willingness
to seek information that challenges our own understandings and an openness to contradictory evidence
– is central to EBP in social work. Processes of falsification lead to inclusiveness and are a check on
biases and blind spots, which is one of the main purposes of the scientific approach and a goal of EBP
(Sheldon, 2001).
(Gilgun, 2005: 52–61)

2. (summary)

Again, look for the words that tell you what the paper *does*.

This paper *considers* the validity of evidence-based practice in social work. It critically *examines* | Writer's argu-
various underlying assumptions entailed in evidence-based practice and *draws out* their implica- | ment: notice
tions for social work. Following a consideration of the background to the development of evidence- ← italicized verbs
based practice and a discussion of its key organizing concepts, the paper goes on to *examine* its | that tell you
underlying scientific assumptions. ... It is *argued* that social workers engage in a reflexive under- | what the paper
standing and not a determinate or certainty based decision-making process based on objective | does.
evidence.
(Webb, 2001: 57–9)

GETTING A GENERAL PICTURE OF THE AREA/TOPIC

Responding critically, asking the right questions, or recognizing the answers, can be difficult if you don't have much idea of the topic or area. The following can be useful in providing an overview:

- Lectures
- Text books
- Review articles in journals
- Editorials in journals
- Book reviews in journals

As an example, consider the following editorial, 'Whose Evidence and for What Purpose' in the journal *Social Work*. It first provides a general picture and then identifies questions, issues, and problems.

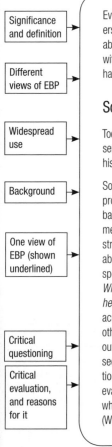

Significance and definition →

Different views of EBP →

Widespread use →

Background →

One view of EBP (shown underlined) →

Critical questioning →

Critical evaluation, and reasons for it →

Evidence-based practice (EBP) is one of the predominant new ways of thinking about what social workers should do in their practice and how they should decide to do it. EBP involves using the 'best available' evidence, often interpreted to mean research-based 'knowledge' about specific types of practices with particular problems. Although its advocates tout EBP as an imperative for social workers, others have raised questions regarding potential drawbacks of this approach.

Social work and EBP

Today, EBP has become a common term in many professions, including social work. Attempts to deal seriously with systematic evidence as a way to reduce uncertainty and improve practice have a long history in social work, …

Social workers' current advocacy or adoption of EBP can be thought of as an expression of the profession's recent attention to research activities and ways of thinking. The idea of systematically basing our practice on scientific evidence is appealing in our 'tell me what works' society. Paralleling medicine to a degree not seen in years, recent concerted efforts to place social work in the mainstream of scientifically oriented professions <u>can be considered the enactment of cultural beliefs</u> about what a profession should do and be. If only we have enough evidence, based on accurate specification of conditions, outcomes, and interventions, we should be able to solve our problems. *What remains unclear is the range and types of problems for which the 'what works' formulation is helpful.* For example, it may be a useful formulation for problems that are believed to exist stably across time and contexts, where problems and interventions can be specified … and replicated in other practice settings, where they exist in deterministic relationships to one another, and where outcome measures are seen as reflecting rather than generating the problems they address. It seemed less useful for a world characterised by shifting, multiple identities and relational constructions, in which an 'outcome' is at most the beginning of something else, where the production and evaluation of knowledge for practice considered mutual activities between professionals and people who use their services.
(Witkin and Harrison, 2001: 293–6)

WHAT DO YOU THINK?

Another useful thing to do when you are taking notes is to note both the relevant point and your first spontaneous response to it. Is it consistent with your experience and your observations? Do you think it makes sense? Don't censor your reaction – just write down whatever it is: sceptical, questioning, interested. Your own experience can often be the beginning – but by no means the end – of developing a critical response. You then have a guide into reading other texts that may express some of the responses you had.

You may find it helpful to take notes on a divided page with plenty of room for your own comments, as well as space to record the bibliographic details (full title, date of publication, page reference, etc.).

SPECIFIC QUESTIONS TO ASK OF THE TEXT

Important questions to begin with are:

- What is the writer's main argument?

  How certain is the writer? Is their argument qualified in any way? Look for words or phrases such as may, might, could (see discussion of modals and certainty in the next chapter).

- What evidence do they provide to support this?

  Is there enough evidence? How strong is it? Where does it come from? What are the limitations of the evidence?

- What methodology do they use?

- What is their theoretical framework?

  Is it appropriate? How do they define key concepts?

- What are their assumptions?

  What are their underlying assumptions? Are they explicitly stated? Consider the following points:

  EBP, like all approaches, is ideological in the sense that it assumes certain beliefs and adheres to certain values. Understanding these assumptions, beliefs, and values requires examining EBP through a variety of lenses (for example, social reform) and questioning what is taken for granted or considered un-problematic. For example, we might question whether there are parallels between EBP's current affiliation with medicine and social work's affiliation with psychiatry in the early part of the twentieth century. What do (did) we gain and what do (did) we lose by this association? Or we might enquire about what EBP-informed social work practice is actually like. How does that position the profession vis-à-vis its social values? What effect will it have on issues of relationship that are so central to social work practice? (Witkin and Harrison, 2001: 294)

- How does the argument apply to real people in specific situations?

  Is it an appropriate theory to apply in a particular context? How does that influence the way the writer considers the topic?

- Does the writer acknowledge other writers' work?
  How do they deal with counter-evidence?
  What are alternative views? Exactly how do they differ? Is that significant? Can you group the various viewpoints in any way? Look for clues to this in the literature as in the Gilgun extract on page 63.

And, most importantly,

- How is it relevant to your assignment topic or question?
  Your purposes will probably be different from those of the writer of a text you are reading. A critical comment might simply be noting the validity of a particular idea or approach, but pointing out that this is limited to a particular situation or context. You can then think whether it is appropriate to the situation you are writing about, whether it can be adapted.
  All the time, keep in mind your purpose in reading and thinking about the text. Are you comparing different analyses or accounts of an issue or situation? Or trying to assess the most effective policy or practice for a specific situation? Or … ?

- What is your personal response?
  How do you feel about it? Does it fit with your own experiences?
  Evaluate in context of your question and purposes.

CRITICAL REVIEWS

Writing a critical review brings together critical thinking, critical analysis of a particular text, and critical writing.

Critical reviews usually (unless specified otherwise by your lecturer) have the following basic structure:

FIRST, AN INTRODUCTORY PARAGRAPH

Here you summarize the writer's main aim and argument. The bibliographic details are often put at the top of the review but, if not, you should mention them in the first sentence. You should also briefly indicate your overall critical response to the article.

SECOND, SUMMARY

Summarize the main points of the book or article but be succinct. This shouldn't take up more than half the review, and could be one-third.

THIRD, CRITICAL COMMENTARY

Discuss the content of the text: the ideas, the arguments, the theory used, the methodology (if appropriate), or whatever is the particular focus of your task. Consider the implication of the points made. Indicate your evaluation of these aspects. Is the text successful in doing what it aimed to do?

Note that these last two sections can be done either sequentially in separate sections or integrated. Often, it's more effective to summarize a point or argument and then discuss it.

FOURTH, CONCLUSION

Here you summarize the article's strengths and weaknesses, and re-state your critical response.

EXAMPLE OF CRITICAL REVIEWS

The following extracts from critical reviews demonstrate the ways in which reviewers summarize the content of a book and then comment critically. Notice the integrated summary and critical commentary.

In order to develop your vocabulary of evaluative language, it's very helpful to browse through the book reviews of social work journals and note the words and phrases, both positive and negative, used. Note the use of modal language (discussed in the next chapter), i.e. words such as *would, could, might.*

EXTRACTS

Introduction: overview, including brief summary and writer's aim.

(1) An edited collection of nine chapters, this is an *ambitious and timely book* drawing upon material from a range of places, including Australia, Britain and continental Europe. …It aims to redress the predominantly urban bias evident in writing on social policy and social welfare. …This text is a *welcome addition to the literature* on rural life, but, as with most edited collections, the *merits of the chapters vary* according to one's predilections and interests. …

> Note critical comments in italics.

> Reviewer's overall response

The third chapter by Warner examines the impact of marketization, privatization and decentralization. … This is an *interesting and informative* discussion, *though readers might contest* Warner's assertion that. … For, as Warner herself notes … [reason for counter-claim]. …

> Summary

Unfortunately, in this chapter, as well as the preface, there is little sustained discussion of globalization, resulting in a relatively uncritical acceptance of the notion, particularly in regard to its theoretical status …

A summarizing conclusion … *would have been valuable.* In addition, some discussion of personal social services and social care … *would have been valuable.*
(Pugh, 2009: 323–4)

> Note use of modal verbs

(2) It is *unclear* if the authors intend each targeted group to take action using the information presented, or if the topics are addressed for contextual understanding. In either case, the authors *do not sufficiently explain the relevance* of each chapter to the specific roles and responsibilities of different readers. … Furthermore, the authors *fail to address sufficiently* the larger structural issues. …
Despite these challenges, the book offers *several important insights.* … The authors *successfully* highlight the influence of. … They *convincingly* demonstrate how assumptions about low-income individuals and communities can lead to …

> Note critical comments

Most notably, the authors emphasize the importance of school and community context in order to understand student behavior and learning. They *provide compelling evidence* that … . *With such well-substantiated observations* ….
(Anyon, 2008: 410–11)

(3) In Chapter 6, quantitative data from the British Household Panel Youth Survey are used to illustrate the effects of poverty on children's experiences of school. Here, Ridge compares the experiences of children in low-income households with those of children from families with adequate income. Since the qualitative data were generated from interviews with children in low-income families, this chapter adds a *valuable comparative dimension* to the book.
(Tipper, 2006: 363)

Summary chapter, followed critical comment

CONCLUSION

This chapter has focused on developing the skills for critical thinking, reading, and writing. The use of extracts from the social work literature as examples suggests an ongoing way in which you can develop both your critical and linguistic skills while simultaneously doing the required reading.

Finding out more

Web links

Most of the university academic writing or communication sites listed at the end of the next chapter have a section on critical thinking and writing. These university based ones are generally more useful than the numerous critical thinking sites with a more corporate approach.

Books

Graff, G. and Birkenstein, C. (2007) *They Say/I Say: The Moves that Matter in Persuasive Writing.* W.W. New York: Norton.

This book helps you with the language skills and rhetorical moves necessary to taking part in the academic conversation.

Wallace, M. and Wray, A. (2006) *Critical Reading and Writing for Postgraduates.* London: SAGE.

Written for postgraduates but useful for final year undergraduates. Provides a thorough and detailed introduction to critical reading and writing, including downloadable resources.

7 ACADEMIC WRITING: MAKING IT WORK

In this chapter, we look at key features of academic writing and suggest strategies for effective and appropriate writing. This will assist you to:

- incorporate a large amount of evidence;
- synthesize information from different sources;
- demonstrate your own perspective;
- write clearly;
- produce a well-structured and cohesive piece of writing.

I was a bit nervous about academic writing.

I found coming from high school, learning to write academically was hard, like what is expected of you and the different things you have to include.

I came to uni really under-prepared. I had never done academic writing before. (SW students)

Academic writing is often daunting for students; they may see it as an ability that some people just seem to have. However, there's nothing magical about writing in an 'academic' style; it's a skill that, like any other, can be acquired. Like any other writing style, such as emails or text messages, it has developed in a particular context with particular features. These features can be identified as you will see below, when we look at certain conventions and characteristics of academic writing, and discuss how to reproduce them in your own writing.

What's required at all stages of the writing process is the same kind of reflexivity that's needed for critical thinking (as discussed in the previous chapter) and, more generally, as a social work student:

… as social work students we are taught to be self-reflective. (SW student)

With regard to writing, you need to be aware of the features of academic writing generally, the specific conventions of your discipline; the requirements of your particular assignment; and the expectations of your reader(s).

It's also often helpful to think of writing as a process, to be aware of what you are trying to do in your writing. Rather than putting the focus on the product (What has to be written?), put the focus on what you are doing (What am I trying to do here?). By focusing on what you are doing – for example, introducing, comparing, summarizing, evaluating – it is easier to identify which linguistic skills are needed.

In this section, and in the following chapter, we outline some of the ways of using language which make it possible for writing to carry out the above functions.

WRITING IN SOCIAL WORK DEGREES

Studying for social work involves different kinds of writing: both the writing which is a preparation for the kinds of writing you will do as a practitioner after you graduate, and the writing in a particular disciplinary subject such as social theory or sociology. While there are basic similarities, each discipline has its conventions of writing. A lot of this is gradually absorbed as you read and write in your undergraduate degree. However, it's often helpful to focus on the writing style and conventions of a particular discipline so that you can speed up the process and write more appropriately for your discipline. An additional issue for social work students is that of integrating material from different disciplines, for example, psychology, but maintaining a social work perspective. Chapter 9 explores issues in writing in social work in more depth.

WRITING IN THE SOCIAL WORK PROFESSION

Writing in social work is concerned with effective professional communication within particular contexts, such as a team or institution. Healy and Mulholland (2007: 13) identify three elements of effective writing: 'awareness of institutional context, professional purpose and audience'. Social workers may be writing with the purpose of communicating within a team, influencing policy, writing records to satisfy accountability requirements, or reporting on programmes (Healy and Mulholland, 2007). The writing required for these purposes is not dissimilar from that required, in a general sense, for academic writing: clear, effective, focused, reasoned, based on evidence, and appropriate to the conventions of the institution and to the characteristics and needs of the audience.

WRITING IN A PARTICULAR DISCIPLINE

The following suggestions are based on Craswell's (2005: 28–30) helpful outline of how to master disciplinary writing practices. First, find a good model of the particular writing task (such as an essay, reflective writing, or report). Ask your lecturer or tutor for models. Or ask them to recommend a well-written article. Then, read it carefully, focusing on the writing not the content. Investigate how the writers do certain things in writing for example:

USING THE MATERIAL

- How writers use theories or research methodologies, i.e. how do they write about and apply them?
- How they incorporate evidence from various sources, including empirical data.

ORGANIZING THE MATERIAL

- How do writers structure their text? Divide it into sections? Use headings and sub-headings?
- How do writers link different parts of the text?
- How do writers structure argument?

WRITING ABOUT THE MATERIAL

- What kind of language do writers in a particular discipline use, for example to discuss, evaluate, criticize? Are certain phrases or words used frequently?

After this close reading and analysis some students find it helpful to note key phrases or expressions, and so build up their own *corpus* of examples of typical and effective disciplinary writing.

KEY FEATURES OF ACADEMIC WRITING

Academic writing is, first of all, writing that is clear and grammatically correct. As well as these characteristics, common to all good writing, it usually has the following features:

- structure and cohesion;
- citation and evidence;
- modality;
- distinctive language style and tone;
- distinctive voice or perspective.

Each of these points is discussed below, with particular focus on how language is used to achieve these features.

STRUCTURE AND COHESION

Academic writing is highly structured, following certain conventions, with possible local variations. Different genres of writing (for example, essays, reports, reflective statements) are expected to be organized in certain ways. Similarly, different sections of a text, such as introductions or conclusions, are structured according to certain conventions. The major kinds of academic writing will be discussed in detail in the next chapter. An important aspect of structure is *cohesion*, i.e. how all the different elements are woven together in a smoothly flowing whole. Cohesion makes it easier for your reader to follow what you are saying. Ways of achieving this are discussed below, in relation to paragraphs, and in the next chapter.

PARAGRAPHS: STRUCTURE AND FEATURES

As well as the macro-structure of a text, there are also expectations about what could be called the micro-structure, and particularly paragraphs. A paragraph is a basic unit of organization in writing (perhaps *the* basic unit in academic writing) in which a group of related sentences develops one main idea. Paragraphs are the main vehicle for developing your argument, explanation or account.

Each paragraph makes one major point, or one component of a single broader point. A paragraph can also be organized around a single function, for example, cause-effect, classification or comparison/contrast, and are written accordingly. The length of a paragraph can vary, but in academic writing they usually comprise 4–7 (average length) sentences. A paragraph must be long enough to develop its main idea adequately.

PARAGRAPH STRUCTURE

- *Topic sentence*

  The topic sentence, usually the first sentence, states what the paragraph is about. It is general enough to encompass all the sentences/points in the paragraph, and specific enough to make a clear point. The link between every sentence in the paragraph and the topic sentence should be clear. The topic sentence should be in your voice, in your words; this is not the place to use quotations or paraphrases of other people's ideas, namely, do not begin a paragraph with 'According to Gardener (2005) …' or 'Gardener (2005) claims that …'

- *Supporting sentences*

  The other sentences, the supporting sentences, develop the topic in a range of ways: explanation, elaboration, illustration, analysis, comparison, etc. The link between every sentence in the paragraph and the topic sentence should be clear.

- *Final sentence*

  The final sentence can be a concluding sentence but is better understood as a 'wrap' sentence: Dunleavy (2003: 112) suggests the 'topic, body, wrap' structure. The wrap sentence(s) is not a simple summary of what you've just said – which would be repetitive and irritating for the reader – but should pull the paragraph together and comment on the significance of its content. It can also link the current paragraph to the next one.

FEATURES OF A PARAGRAPH

A paragraph is unified and cohesive: i.e. it is built around one main idea and the different parts of the paragraph are connected to each other so that the whole paragraph is woven together.

Some of the linking devices are:

- *Transition signals*

    Transition signals are words or phrases which link sentences and paragraphs so that the writing flows smoothly. They function like signposts in the text, and indicate the writer's organization or thinking or intentions. Transition signals are discussed in detail in Chapter 8 in relation to the structure of essay and report writing.

- *Repetition*

    Repetition of key words or phrases within a paragraph and between paragraphs, note that the words don't have to be in exactly the same form, but can refer to an idea or thing previously mentioned in the paragraph.

- *This/these + summary word*

    For example:

    > However, it can be seen in Table 2 that while 33 per cent are poor on at least one dimension, only 5.7 per cent are poor on all three measures simultaneously. *These results* indicate a considerable lack of overlap between measures that have been, and are still used to represent poverty. (Bradshaw and Finch, 2003: 516)

- *Parallelism*

    Parallelism refers to the use of similar grammatical structures for similar elements of meaning within a sentence or among sentences. Parallelism connects the different parts of a sentence, as well as the sentences of a paragraph, so that the writing flows more smoothly and is more easily understood. For example:

    > These studies have focused community attention on the need to *assess* the adequacy of income support payments, *tackle* the root causes of poverty (e.g. unemployment and discrimination), and *address* its consequences (e.g. social alienation, restricted child development and poor health outcomes). (Saunders et al., 2008: 176)

    The parallel structure in the above sentence shows the relation between the three italicized words, all referring to actions that there is a *need* to take. Note that they are parallel in structure but don't necessary correspond word for word.

    Parallel structures are useful when comparing or contrasting:

    > There are two distinct ways in which to reflect on the meaning of poverty. …The first *concerns what poverty means to those who study it;* the second *emphasises what poverty means to those who experience it.* The first approach *has dominated* the poverty literature and *has focused* on how to set a poverty line. (Saunders, 2003: 4)

Parallelism should also be used for lists, and for headings in essays. Note that in the following example the basic parallel structure is that each item is a gerund (-ing form of the verb) followed by an adjective and noun:

There are many ways we can encourage collaboration between service workers and service users. These include:

- Promoting a collaborative physical environment.
- Promoting a collaborative interpersonal relationship.
- Encouraging collaborative and creative solution seeking. (Healy, 2005: 162–3)

SAMPLE PARAGRAPH

Topic sentence (shown in bold)		Body of paragraph:
Repetition of key words (underlined)		Elaboration of main idea
Transition signals (shown in *italics*)		'Wrap' sentence

There are two distinct ways in which to reflect on the meaning of poverty (Saunders 2002). *The first* concerns what poverty means to those who **study** it; the *second* emphasizes what poverty means to those who experience it. *The first* approach has dominated the poverty literature and has focused on how to set a poverty line. *The second* meaning of poverty is important because it addresses the impact of poverty and is *thus* inextricably linked with its consequences. It is now widely acknowledged that the definition and measurement of poverty cannot be determined independently of prevailing social conditions, including the ways in which various types of hardship are perceived and measured. Poverty is *thus* relative in the sense that the resources required to avoid hardship will depend upon social conditions, but this is still consistent with a measure of deprivation that is absolute in relation to capabilities (Sen, 1995).

| Link between paragraphs |

Poverty is also relative in another sense. ...
(Saunders, 2003: 4–5)

CITATION AND EVIDENCE

The use of evidence, providing information that supports your point, and citation, quoting or attributing a statement to a writer or speaker, are among the most distinctive features of academic writing. Citing other scholars' work can give authority to your writing. It also enables you to take a position in relation to other writing (Giltrow, 2005).

Using evidence and citation requires skills in paraphrasing, summarizing, and quoting (discussed below) as well as the ethical issues involved (see the next chapter).

Use other people's work critically (as discussed in the previous chapter). You read it for your purposes because you want to explain something or find a useful methodology or to find a particular bit of information. And when you write you *incorporate* it into your essay. There are three ways of doing this: summarizing, paraphrasing, and quoting.

SUMMARIZING, PARAPHRASING AND QUOTING: THE BASICS

SUMMARIZING

A summary contains the main points of a text but omits the supporting or elaborating material. For example, it does not include details or examples.

When you summarize:

- Make sure that you paraphrase other people's words.
- Use summaries of other people's writing, of events, or of spoken words as evidence in constructing your argument.
- Include an interpretive and/or evaluative comment on the point(s) that you have summarized.

Tips for summarizing

- Read carefully and identify the main points.
- Write the main points in note form, excluding all details. Follow the suggestions for paraphrasing (below).
- Write the summary in sentence form.
- Revise, check that you have included all the main points, and that it is in your own words.

EXAMPLE

The following example is typical of the kind of summary that is required in academic writing. Often it's necessary to summarize several pages or a chapter in a few sentences. See Saunders et al., (2008: 177–9) for the full text.

> In summary, while the deprivation approach has been used to better identify poverty, social exclusion offers an alternative that opens up broader issues associated with the role of institutional structures and processes in promoting or impeding rights and responsibilities. Both concepts are related to poverty, but these links have been developed in different ways and been given different emphases. (Saunders et al., 2008: 179)

PARAPHRASING

Paraphrasing is expressing another writer's idea in your own words. It seems straightforward but in practice it is often quite difficult. Many students find it hard to maintain their own voice when paraphrasing, sometimes because they feel that the original writer expressed it so well. Nevertheless, it is important to put something in your own words; otherwise, you run the risk of plagiarizing.

When you paraphrase:

- Read the section of text to be paraphrased several times. Make sure you have a good understanding of it.
- Write down the main points of the text WITHOUT looking at it.
- Check that your paraphrase is correct.
- Write the paraphrase in your own words making sure:
  - that the meaning is the same and you give the same relative importance to each point as in the original;
  - that the attitude to the topic – for example, critical, questioning – is the same as in the original.
- Check that your text is an accurate paraphrase of the original.

Note: specialized words are not paraphrased: for example, you wouldn't need to paraphrase *census*.

Language tips for paraphrasing

- Use synonyms, i.e. words which have a similar meaning. However, a change of context can lead to a shift in the meaning of a word so be careful. If you use a thesaurus check the dictionary as well.
- Change the voice of the verb from active to passive or vice versa.
- Change the grammatical form of a word, e.g. from verb to noun (see nominalization below).

ORIGINAL

It [mindfulness] posits that physicians must be aware of their own cultural and religious values if they are to be responsive to patients. (Gilgun, 2005: 54)

PARAPHRASE

According to the concept of mindfulness, sensitivity to the needs of patients requires reflection by medical practitioners upon their personal cultural and religious beliefs (Gilgun, 2005).

QUOTING

When you quote you reproduce written or spoken words. The words and the punctuation are exactly the same as in the original and are enclosed within quotation marks.

When you quote:

Make the point first in your own words and then use the quotation to support it: to give it more authority, to express it in a particularly eloquent and memorable way, or to let the voice of someone else be heard (e.g. a client in social work).

Don't quote because you're tired and can't be bothered constructing the sentence yourself. That's when your voice fades out.

Make clear to your reader why you have included the quote: explain the significance of it. For every line of quotation you should have a line of commentary or interpretation.

Tips for quoting

- Introduce a quotation with a colon (:) or comma, depending on the sentence structure.
- Don't just include a sentence of quotation without any introduction.
- Start a quotation longer than three lines on a new line (following a colon in the previous one) and indent it.
- If you want to omit any words you show this by an elipsis, i.e. three dots …
- Indicate a quotation within a quoted passage by single inverted commas (if double quotation marks are used for the passage) or vice versa.

REPORTING A WRITER'S WORDS OR ACTIONS (BOTH PARAPHRASE AND QUOTATION)

A range of verbs is used in reporting what a writer has said or done. In choosing a word make sure that it is appropriate to the context, and accurately reflects the writer's meaning and intention. You can indicate that the writer is making a statement (says, comments, states), arguing a position (argues, claims) has a positive attitude (supports, agrees), or a negative attitude (criticizes, dismisses) towards their subject, or indicate the writers' degree of certainty (questions, suggests, insists).

Generally, the present tense is used when introducing a writer's words or thoughts, e.g. argues, comments, describes. However, if you are referring to what someone actually *did* in the past you use the simple past tense, e.g. surveyed, interviewed, found (on the basis of research).

Consider the effect of different reporting verbs in the following extracts:

Reid and Epstein *encouraged* social workers to draw thoughtfully on a broad range of theoretical perspectives … (Healy, 2005: 112).

British social theorist Mark Doel (1998: 197) *contends* that the task-centred approach has moved into 'more radical territory …' (Healy, 2005: 112).

Doel and Marsh (1992: 106) *assert* that this is 'a departure from the grand reformism of social work in bygone days. …' (Healy, 2005: 113).

Trotter (1999: 48) *suggests* that the themes that should be addressed … (Healy, 2005: 118).

Commonly used verbs include (in addition to the ones mentioned above) the following:

- agree
- acknowledge
- add
- assert
- conclude
- contend
- demonstrate
- describe
- explain
- identify
- imply
- infer
- mention
- note
- observe
- report
- remark
- point out
- see
- show
- suggest

It's important to summarize, paraphrase, and quote other people's work with integrity so that you fairly represent what they are saying, and give due acknowledgment. Make sure it's clear what's yours and what's theirs. (See referencing section in next chapter for further discussion of the ethical issues involved.)

MODALITY (ALSO DISCUSSED IN RELATION TO WRITER'S VOICE BELOW)

Modality is a linguistic term which refers to a writer's attitude towards the truth of a statement; that is, whether s/he thinks that the statement is certain, probable, or possible. This can be expressed through verbs such as *must, can, could, may, might, appears, seems, suggests, indicates*; and in adjectives and adverbs such as *certain(ly), probable/probably, possible/possibly, apparently, perhaps*. As well as indicating probability and possibility, modal words can also indicate obligation and advisability. These are expressed through verbs such as *must, should, might*.

The use of modalized statements is characteristic of much academic writing and reflects the complexity of questions and the limitations of knowledge. It also highlights 'the sense of the statement in which it occurs as being knowledge under construction from a certain location: the speaker's or writer's position in the world' (Giltrow, 2005: 217). The use of modal expressions is also due to the need for rigour and care, namely thinking about what your evidence allows you to say. The following examples indicate some of the uses of modality:

> In the domain of human relationships, then, professional talk centres not so much on uncertainty, but on complex characterizations. These formulations *may* or *may not* be accompanied by references to specific theories. That is, the popular nature of the ideas invoked *apparently* exempts practitioners from the imperative to justify their actions using formal knowledge. In the slippery world of relationships and interaction professionals *seem* to suspend disbelief, whilst in more rational-technical activities they *seem* to be *more likely* to display scepticism. (White, 2009: 227)

Modality is clearly relevant to the discipline of social work, of which one of the 'legitimating narratives' is critical reflexivity (White, 2009: 223). Spafford et al., see the question of uncertainty and how it is regarded as 'central' (2007: 157). They cite Brashers' (2001) description of uncertainty as occurring when 'details of situations are ambiguous, complex, unpredictable, or probabilistic; when information is unavailable or inconsistent; and when people feel insecure in their own state of knowledge or the state of knowledge in general' (p.157).

Consider the following examples:

> These results indicate that accumulation *might* be a better way of using overlapping measures of poverty than by giving priority to one dimension or another. (Bradshaw and Finch, 2003: 513)

> They are *likely* to be experiencing a harsher degree of poverty than those poor on any one of the measures. They are therefore *perhaps* a priority for policy. (Bradshaw and Finch, 2003: 515)

> Depending on the medical situation, one type of knowledge may carry more weight than another. (Gilgun, 2005: 55)

> I *suggest* that there are four cornerstones of EBP in social work: … (Gilgun, 2005: 59)

When writing as a social work practitioner in reports or case records, it is important to indicate where you are certain of your facts and where not (Healy and Mulholland, 2007). As well as explicitly stating your doubts you can also indicate this by using modalized language such as:

> The 5-year-old son *appears* to have been present during frequent parental quarrels … (Healy and Mulholland, 2007: 92)

The use of the word 'appears' tells the reader that the writer believes the child to have been present but cannot state that for certain.

ACADEMIC STYLE

Academic writing has a more formal tone, partly as a result of the need to be precise and accurate in its statements. The following examples of language use, adapted from Swales and Feak (2004) contribute to this more formal tone.

VOCABULARY

- Using a single verb rather than a verb + preposition: for example, compare *investigate* to *look into*. Other such formal/informal pairs are: *constitute/make up; eliminate or abolish/get rid of.*
- Using more formal words rather than more colloquial alternatives. For example, use *considerable* rather than *a lot of; achieved, gained,* or *obtained* rather than *got.*

GRAMMAR

- Using more formal negative forms rather than the (equally grammatically correct) informal ones. Use *few* instead of *not many, little* instead of *not much.*
- Avoiding rhetorical questions: while rhetorical questions are frequently used in academic speaking, including formal presentations, they are generally not used in academic writing. They tend to interrupt the flow of the argument, and contribute little.
- Avoiding the use of contractions such as *don't, won't*, etc. Write *do not, will not.*

USING NOMINALIZATION

Nominalization – changing verbs into nouns – is another writing tool that can be very useful in academic writing, but needs to used with care. It can be useful for condensing information into one word rather than a whole clause; this is especially useful in academic writing where you need to synthesize large amounts of information, and include a lot in a sentence. It's also appropriate for dealing with abstract ideas. However, as Kamler and Thomson (2006) point out, the effects of nominalization are not neutral because nominalization can obscure agency and thus responsibility in a statement. Their example (2006: 109) demonstrates this:

The detonation of an atomic bomb in Hiroshima resulted in widespread mortality.

When American planes *detonated* the atomic bomb in Hiroshima, thousands of Japanese civilians *died*.

In the first sentence it is not stated who caused the action, or who suffered the consequences. However, in the second sentence, the use of verbs makes clear the subjects and objects of the action. The example from Healy and Mulholland's (2007) text, cited on page 82, makes clear the importance of attribution of agency and responsibility.

THE PASSIVE VOICE

The use of the passive voice – where the object of the action is the subject of the sentence, and the person carrying out the action is not the subject – is a question of writing style. Students are frequently advised, on the one hand, that the passive voice is characteristic of academic writing and, on the other hand, that it should be avoided. However, using the passive voice, or not, depends on the context and writing purpose. The passive may be appropriate in the following instances:

- When the agent of the action is not known or it's not necessary for the agent to be known.
- When the writer wants to put the focus on issues, not individual people. This can be related to the idea of theme/rheme which is discussed below.
- When the writer wants to avoid a personal tone.

However, there are also many occasions when it is important that the agent be known, or to make clear that the writer is stating her/his position. In addition, excessive use of the passive voice can make writing very dull or force the writer into long-winded, indirect statements.

THEME/RHEME

The first part of a sentence or clause (before the verb) is the theme (a term from linguistics, not the usual meaning of the word). The rest of the sentence is the rheme. Generally, what you put in the theme of a sentence is what gets most prominence. If you want to put the focus on a certain point, put it in the theme.

The following two sentences illustrate this shift in the focus of a sentence:

Deprivation is represented here by a lack of socially perceived necessities. (Bradshaw and Finch, 2003: 515)

Socially perceived necessities here represent deprivation.

The question of whether to put something in the theme or rheme of a sentence is also related to linking sentences. A new idea that is introduced in the rheme of a sentence, can then be developed further by putting it in the theme of the next sentence:

For example:

It [this article] is an exploration of different measures of poverty made possible by the Survey of Poverty and Social Exclusion in Britain. This survey was a national follow-up survey in 1999 of about 1300 households who were respondents to the 1998/99 General Household Survey. (Bradshaw and Finch, 2003: 515)

See Kamler and Thomson (2006) for a detailed and extremely helpful discussion of theme and rheme.

MAKING YOUR VOICE HEARD IN YOUR ACADEMIC WRITING

A writing voice can be as distinctive as a speaking voice. However, in academic writing it's often difficult to synthesize all the ideas you're hearing and reading about, as well as what you're learning through placement experience, and work out what you think and to 'have a sense of entitlement to have ideas and to write about them' (Rudestam and Newton, 2001: 213). It is easy for that voice to be swamped by other louder, more confident voices that you bring in from the texts you use. In addition, fears of plagiarism often lead students to go to the other extreme and give excessive prominence to their sources. There are various ways, outlined below, of making your voice heard; which ones you choose depend on your subject and its conventions, your particular purpose at that point in the text, and the kind of writing.

USING THE FIRST PERSON

Many students think that the best way to make your voice heard is simply by using the first person: *I think*, *in my opinion* and so on. However, the use of the first person is a complicated question, regarded differently in different disciplines. Conventions, which discourage the use of the first person, have been critiqued as portraying a pseudo-objectivity or down-playing the possibility of other interpretations.

In a professional social work context, Healy and Mulholland point out that while writing in the third person seems more objective there are also advantages to writing in the first person:

> [Y]ou can be more direct writing in the first person and, because of the relationship-based nature of social work practice, writing in the first person can appear more consistent with the material you represent. It can be difficult, for example, to sustain the position of third person when discussing a situation in which you have had sustained professional involvement. (Healy and Mulholland, 2007: 92)

They provide the following example of an occasion where the statement involved the writer's experience and also needed to make clear that the information was the writer's interpretation:

> The 5-year-old son appears to have been present during frequent parental quarrels, and I witnessed two occasions where he fled the room crying. (Healy and Mulholland, 2007: 92)

Using 'I' is particularly helpful when you want to:

- Tell the reader how you have organized your writing or why you have organized it in a particular way, or your intentions in doing so. This is called the authorial and is most commonly used in introductory sections. For example:

  > I thought it may be useful to articulate the differences and attempt, where possible, to generate some explanations for them. (White 2009: 223)

- Report on how you have carried out research. For example:

  > My ideas on this matter developed substantially whilst I was analysing a corpus of data from a two-year ethnographic study of an integrated child health service ... (White, 2009: 224)

Although notice how the writer then switches to the third person:

> Methods included observation of clinics, ward rounds and staff/team meetings, audio-recording of interprofessional talk ... , the tracking of a number of individual cases ... (White, 2009: 224)

- Talk about your own experiences or feelings. This is particularly relevant in reporting on a professional experience (as in the example above) as well as in reflective writing which requires you to include a personal response. See the examples in the section on reflective writing in Chapter 9.

However, there are disadvantages to using 'I' or to using it too much:

- It states the obvious: it is your essay so the arguments and ideas are yours.
- It is repetitive and can be tedious.
- It takes the focus off the point. Rather than getting straight into the point or argument at the beginning of the sentence (the theme, see page 81) you waste this space.

However, if you do use 'I' to make your point or state your argument it's best to use it in a limited way and, again, particularly in introductions or conclusions. While there is certainly a place for using the first person, it is not always the most effective way to communicate your ideas in academic writing. There are other ways – discussed below – which are often more appropriate and effective. Most importantly, you should check with your lecturer to find out what the convention in your particular subject/course is with regard to using the first person 'I'.

WRITING TECHNIQUES TO MAKE YOUR VOICE HEARD

Below are some suggestions for ways you can do this that keep your voice strong and clear.

ORGANIZING THE MATERIAL

You choose the books, articles, and reports to read. Many of them will come from reading lists or your lecturer's suggestions but you also can find other texts. Follow up your particular interests or point of view. Get references from bibliographies, scan journals, or the library shelves.

ARGUING A POSITION

You take a position, state it clearly, and elaborate it throughout an essay, making sure that you are consistent. See the next chapter for discussion of this.

TOPIC SENTENCES

Topic sentences (see above) are one of the most effective ways of making your argument clear throughout the essay. Each topic sentence states another point, or sub-point, in the development of your argument. Topic sentences should be in your voice, in your words; this is not the place to use quotations or paraphrases of other people's ideas. You can do that in the rest of the paragraph.

THEME/RHEME

Generally, what you put in the theme of a sentence is what gets most prominence. If you want to put the focus on a certain point, put it in the theme. The themes of sentences throughout a paragraph have a strong effect on the overall impression the reader gets of the content. If you put all the emphasis on other writers your voice and argument disappear.

WRITING ABOUT YOUR WRITING (WHAT'S KNOWN AS META-DISCOURSE)

The use of transition signals and other markers in your writing also helps your voice to be heard, as well as linking sentences and paragraphs. You can use them to tell the reader how you've organized the writing (*firstly, secondly*) or what you are doing (*for example, in contrast*). See the examples above.

USING THE EVIDENCE

You select the appropriate evidence and direct the reader to it, signalling, for example, where the evidence is in agreement with your point of view and where it presents an opposing position. For example:

> Poverty is also relative in another sense. In a famous passage from *The Wealth of Nations*, Adam Smith equates poverty with a lack of necessities, ... Peter Townsend *similarly* refers to people being poor when they lack whatever is 'customary or at least widely encouraged or approved, in the societies to which they belong' ... *In both examples*, the emphasis on custom implies a degree of conformity with social conditions and expectations that extends beyond material resources. (Saunders, 2003: 5)

Notice how the writer uses the evidence to back up his point made in the first (topic) sentence *in his own words*. He directs the reader's attention to the similarity in the examples as well as to the way they support his point.

REPORTING OTHER PEOPLE'S WRITING

In the previous section we discussed how to report on other writers' work. When reporting, it's important to think about how much prominence you want to give your sources; that is, whether you want your voice or their voice to dominate. Contrast, for example, sentence (a) an author prominent citation, and sentence (b) an idea (i.e. the writer's idea) prominent citation.

(a) The concept of poverty has been the focus of intensive research and examination in many countries (Ravaillon, 1996). (Saunders, 2003: 1)

(b) Ravaillon (1996) notes that the concept of poverty has been the focus of intensive research and examination in many countries. (Adapted from Saunders, 2003: 1)

Both ways are appropriate. It depends on the context and what you want to say. However, too many author prominent citations will undermine your voice and interfere with the flow of your argument.

As well, you can choose words that indicate your attitude to their work. If you do use these words you should also demonstrate why they are justified. For example the following adjectives and adverbs have positive connotations: *relevant, useful, significant* (NB: *significant* is used both in a general sense and in a specific way in statistical research). Words with negative connotations, such as *limited, flawed, unhelpful*, are used much less frequently.

As discussed above you can use also modal verbs and modal expressions to indicate your attitude to the subject under discussion: how certain, probable, possible or advisable you think it is.

CONCLUSION

This chapter has focused on the writing appropriate for academic work in social work degrees, aiming to develop the skills required for different kinds of writing tasks. In the next chapter we discuss the features and requirements of particular writing tasks, such as essays and reports.

Finding out more

Web links

Many universities have academic skills resources on a wide range of topics available online. Most also have links to other sites. Following is a selection of particularly useful ones.

University of New South Wales, The Learning Centre, Online Academic Skills Resources:
http://www.lc.unsw.edu.au/olib.html

Academic Skills and Learning Centre, The Australian National University:
https://academicskills.anu.edu.au/

James Cook University, Learning Skills:
http://www.jcu.edu.au/learningskills/

(Continued)

(Continued)

The University of Melbourne, Academic Skills Unit:
http://www.services.unimelb.edu.au/asu/

Purdue University, The Purdue Online Writing Lab:
http://owl.english.purdue.edu/

Sussex Language Institute, University of Sussex:
http://www.sussex.ac.uk/languages/1-6-8.html

Edinburgh Napier University, getting ready for university study:
http://www2.napier.ac.uk/getready/index.html

University of Strathclyde, writing and academic study skills:
http://www.strath.ac.uk/elt/usefullinks/writingacademicstudyskills/

Lancaster University, Lancaster University Library:
http://libweb.lancs.ac.uk/studyskills.htm

Books

There is a vast, widely available literature of academic writing guides. Here are a couple of general guides as well as books dealing with more specific areas.

Craswell, G. (2005) *Writing for Academic Success: A Postgraduate Guide*. London: SAGE.

> Written for postgraduate students but could also be suitable for final year undergraduates. Also included here for the section of disciplinary writing practices, discussed earlier in this chapter.

Fogarty, M. (2008) *Grammar Girl's Quick and Dirty Tips for Better Writing*. New York: Henry Holt.

> As the title suggests, this is a very accessible and readable text but also very helpful guide to grammar.

Graff, G. and Birkenstein, C. (2007) *They say/I say: The Moves That Matter in Persuasive Writing*. New York: W.W. Norton.

> This book helps you with the language skills, such as summary writing, and rhetorical moves necessary to taking part in the academic conversation.

Morley-Warner, T. (2009) *Academic writing is… A Guide to Writing in a University Context*. Sydney: Association for Academic Language and Learning

> A clear and extremely useful guide to the genres of academic writing and the skills required.

Oshima, A. and Hogue, A. (2006) Writing Academic English, 4th edn. Pearson New York: Longman.

> Not new, but still an excellent guide to academic writing, particularly for new undergraduates.

8

ESSAY AND REPORT WRITING: GETTING THE WORDS ONTO THE PAGE

In this chapter we look at two common forms of academic writing in social work: the essay and the report. We aim to help you to:

- understand the writing process and how to do it;
- plan for written work;
- structure essays and reports;
- use evidence and referencing;
- edit and proof-read.

One of the biggest difficulties I found was learning how to structure my essays and assignments ... I found that breaking them down into segments ... helps so much because you then have a structure into which you can write. (SW student)

Throughout the course [you need skills] in writing an essay, in structuring an essay, in doing a report, in doing whatever it is and [this] can comprise quite a significant proportion of the marks in every essay. (SW student)

Putting what you have learnt into writing is often difficult; it is one thing to understand the many new concepts you are learning but putting what you know into writing can seem like a completely different task altogether. As is often said: 'I know the answer, but I just can't get it down on paper'. This is complicated by our level of investment in our own writing; writing represents us in both senses of the word. Writing becomes an extension of ourselves as it stands in for us. Perhaps this is one of the reasons why, as well as being daunting, writing is simultaneously a very rewarding activity. Good written communication is not just a scholarly skill, but, as we explore in the next chapter, a professional skill. You will improve your writing over the term of your degree but there is only one way to do this: by writing.

In this chapter we look at two common forms of academic writing in social work: the essay and the report. But before we get to these genres we look at the overall process of producing a written assignment. Although we tend to think of essays and reports as objects or products, which of course they are, they are, at one and the same time, the products of an elaborate process. Indeed, one thing that you may underestimate is the amount of time it takes to produce a written assignment; in fact we discussed this in Chapter 2.

WRITING AS PROCESS

If you think of writing as a process then it can be broken down into stages. When you look at all these different stages you can perhaps see why lecturers and tutors are forever telling you not to leave everything until the night before the assignment is due.

ASSIGNMENT WRITING STAGES

- Decode the question (identify task).
- Develop provisional thesis or point of view.
- Research.
- Take notes.
- Write plan (includes point of view (POV), content, and structure).
- Write first draft (but may need more than just one).
- Edit and redraft.
- Proof-read (including the references).
- Submit.

Although these stages are listed in a particular sequence, it would be wrong to see essay or report writing as a strictly linear process. At any point you may have to return to a previous stage. So, while you are writing a first draft you may discover that you have insufficient evidence, a weakness you must remedy by returning to the research stage. It is also useful to remember that at any time during a semester you will be working on a number of assignments, which means that you'll be at different stages of this process across a number of assignments. Very rarely will you ever have the luxury of working on just one assignment at a time.

PLANNING YOUR WRITTEN WORK

Many students don't plan their assignments. Writing a plan requires you to think about the essay or report a number of weeks in advance. Therefore, good planning requires good time management – writing an assignment the night before it is due means that you have no time to plan. But when you look at the benefits that good planning can bring to the writer, it is difficult to understand why people might leave it so late. Good plans can save you much time. Good plans will also allow you do justice to your ideas.

WHAT CAN A GOOD PLAN HELP YOU TO DO?

A plan will help you conceive of the task within the word limit. Writing a 3,000 word draft and then judiciously editing it to 1,500 words is really a waste of time. As mentioned, you will likely be working on a number of assignments simultaneously so time spent writing an excessive number of words for one report represents time that can't be spent on another.

As part of the planning process you may have to produce a number of plans, each one more developed and detailed than its predecessor. It is much easier to redraft a plan than an essay. Plans allow you to 'audition' different possible answers to the question so that your final essay, or report, is your best answer, not your first answer. Without a plan your written work will most probably lack focus and direction, and it may even become repetitive. It may also not answer the question or fulfil the task.

A plan allows you to impose your own structure over the material, rather than allowing the material to place its frame over your thinking. Without a good plan it is possible that you will become the intellectual prisoner of the sources you are using. This is especially the case if you have not done enough research.

Time spent planning your essay or report will allow you to write the essay or report in any order. A good plan allows you to be flexible and this flexibility will again save you time.

What details does a useful plan include?

- Provisional thesis or POV/problem to be investigated/hypothesis to be tested.
- Points that could become sections/paragraphs – what issues are you going to raise?
- How many main points will you need to make?
- Sequence of points – in what order are you going to raise them?
- Sources/research that you will draw on to support the points made.

ANALYSING THE QUESTION, DEFINING THE TASK

Regardless of the assignment, your first task is always to answer the question, or to complete the task assigned to you. It does not matter whether you are a skilful writer or a good researcher, or both, if you do not answer the question or complete the correct task, then you have made a fundamental mistake. Moreover, such a failure might indicate that you have missed some vital element of the course because essay questions are normally designed to direct students to investigate important issues. You also find that attendance at lectures and active tutorial participation also makes it easier for you to understand the question. If, after reflection, you still do not understand what you have to do, then speak to your tutor or lecturer before launching yourself into your research.

ANSWERING THE QUESTION

This might seem obvious but students fail to answer the question when they don't draw on the right content. But then, even if you do write about the right concept or issue you can still do so in the wrong way. That is why you need to identify the task word in the question: look out for words like 'discuss', 'outline', 'analyse' and so on. If a question asks you to 'outline the ethics of social work' it is not the same as one that requires an analysis of those ethics. You also need to take into account any limitations that the question imposes. If a question asks you to analyse the ethics of social work in regard to working with children and you analyse ethics generally, then you will not answer the question even if the content of your essay is actually correct.

ESSAY WRITING

Like all genres of writing, an academic essay is highly conventionalized in style and structure. These writing conventions control the way in which you may present your ideas (Clanchy and Ballard, 1991: 52), and often such conventions are not made explicit: when a lecturer sets an essay based assignment he or she expects their students to know what an essay is. Writing a good essay is, therefore, not only about having the right knowledge; it is about putting that knowledge into an acceptable form. Moreover, conventions of academic writing are also conventions of academic reading; the readers of your essays, your markers, will have expectations that you will write in a particular way.

ESSAY STRUCTURE

Essays have three well defined parts: introduction, body and conclusion. Each of these parts has a specific role to play in the overall success of the essay. Put simply, in the introduction you tell the reader what you are going to tell them; in the body you tell them; and in the conclusion you tell the reader what you told them. If this seems a particularly rigid formula then you are right. However, within these quite strict parameters you might be surprised at the degree of choice you have as a writer; essay writing is a much more creative enterprise than you might at first think.

WRITING INTRODUCTIONS

An essay's introduction has two important tasks: it indicates the shape of the overall discussion and it clearly articulates your point of view. A secondary meaning of the word 'essay' is to attempt or try, and in an academic essay you are attempting or trying to convince the reader of something. However, without a clear introduction, your reader knows neither what you are attempting nor how you are going to attempt it. Or to put it another way: reading an essay with a poor introduction or no introduction is akin to arriving at a cinema 20 minutes late for a film; you can work out what's going on but it takes a lot of effort and you are never quite certain that you are following the story properly.

What are the different parts of an essay's introduction?

- Background (what the essay is about).
- Purpose (what the essay will do).
- Thesis statement (POV).
- Outline (points that you will raise in the body).
- Scope (parameters of the overall discussion: sometimes chosen by the writer, sometimes imposed by the question itself. These often make answering the question a more straightforward task).

WRITING BODIES

The body of an essay is comprised of a number of paragraphs that present your argument in a particular order. Paragraphs are the building blocks of your essay. In a short essay of approximately 1,000 words you may not have the space to cover more than four or five points, and each of these points would consume a paragraph. When you write longer essays, however, you might find that you still have a relatively limited number of main points but these main points will be spread across a number of paragraphs; the main points are subdivided into sub-points (paragraphs).

BODY AS A *SEQUENCE*, NOT JUST A *STRUCTURE*

Too often students present essays where the individual paragraphs are good but they are undermined by their illogical sequence. So while you are developing your paragraphs, do so with an eye to how they relate to each other, and the overall purpose of the essay. If you are going to write a cohesive argument then you must also take into account the sequence of paragraphs. In this way, when writing an essay you take on a role similar to that of a film director. You need to ask yourself the question: in what order does the reader need to read these paragraphs in order to best understand the overall point that I am making?

Four common sequences:

- 'General ➔ specific' – a common way to structure body: you start with large scale concerns, and then the essay narrows in focus as it proceeds (for example, you might start by outlining a general problem before moving to offer a specific solution).
- 'General ➔ specific ➔ general' – where you begin with large scale issues (a theory, a definition, a policy, etc.), then focus closely on very specific consideration (a case study for example) before then returning to the large scale concerns.
- 'Then ➔ now' – where you begin at an appropriate place in the past and finish in the present. This is useful when an essay question asks you to 'account for', 'trace', or 'outline' the development or evolution of a phenomenon, issue, or activity.
- 'Problem ➔ solution' – where you divide (but not necessarily equally) the essay between outlining the problem or issue before moving on to offer a solution or remedy.

By arranging your points/paragraphs in a particular order, the body of your essay will be much more cohesive.

WRITING CONCLUSIONS

In the conclusion you have three tasks to fulfil. First, you should refer back to the question you have been asked or the issue you have investigated, but when you do this try to avoid simply repeating the question or your introduction.

Second, your conclusion has to draw together the main points you have raised in the body. So, in part the conclusion should be a summary of the essay as a whole. This means that you no longer need to argue the point, or provide evidence for your claims. A reader will expect to read no new material in your conclusion; if a piece of information is important then it should be in the body.

Third, you need to restate your thesis, major finding or solution.

What goes in a conclusion?

- returns to essay question/task;
- restates thesis (POV);
- recaps outline of main points.
- Note that the conclusion does NOT provide any new evidence.

Importantly, the conclusion and the introduction should be strongly correlated. A common mistake is to write an introduction and conclusion that read like they belong to different essays. This can come about if you start writing your essay without a clear plan: your argument actually changes as you are writing. Other than planning well, one way to ensure that you do not make such a mistake is to write the introduction and the conclusion together at the end of the writing process. In any case, you will almost certainly need to revise the introduction.

REPORT WRITING

Essays are not the only type of written assignment that you will be expected to write. Whereas an essay is very much a form of scholarly writing aimed specifically for assessment, a report, although used as form of assessment, is also a professional writing genre that you will encounter outside the university. It is a form of written communication that is used in many other places and professions, in private industry and the public sector, so time spent writing reports at university is good preparation for the type of writing you will do as a social work practitioner. With this in mind it might be useful to imagine that you are writing your report, not only for your tutor or lecturer, but for a wider audience of social work practitioners.

Sometimes you will hear someone describe a report as 'an essay with headings' and although there are many similarities between the two, there are many important differences. So, do not write an essay when the assignment task requires you to write a report, and vice versa. A report is an account of an investigation into a problem, activity, or topic with suggestion for change of future action. Unlike an essay, which is more organic in structure, a report presents information in a manner that is easily accessible and extractable by the reader, hence the proliferation of headings denoting sections and sub-sections that are the most immediate feature of a report. The longer the report, the more sections and subsections it will have. The accessibility of a report is also achieved through its written style which is precise and economical. You can go a long way to achieving this by leaving out unnecessary details and using direct language.

Structure of a report

Title page
Statement of originality
Executive summary
Acknowledgements
Contents
List of figures and tables
List of symbols and definitions
Introduction
Main sections

    i)   review of literature
    ii) method
    iii) findings

Conclusions and recommendations
Bibliography
Appendices

REPORT STRUCTURE

Whereas an essay can only be divided structurally into three sections, a report has far more constituent parts. You might also find that reports cause different problems because they are more rigidly structured that essays. Beyond the introduction/body/conclusion trinity, you have quite a lot of flexibility when structuring an essay, whereas when writing a report 'the format has the advantage of freeing you from the writer's usual obligation to find a suitable structure for the raw material ...', because 'report writers ... work within a prefabricated structure' (Peters, 1985: 70). In report-writing then there is much less flexibility, however once you have learnt to structure a report correctly you will be able to use the same structure for a number of different assignments, which cannot probably be said about an essay.

Most reports can be divided into four sections.

1   *Preliminaries*

Before you get to the main points of your report there are a numbers of sections that you need to provide. On a *title page* you must provide some basic information including the title of the reports, the names of the authors and the date of submission. After this title page comes the *executive summary*. As its name suggests, it provides a very short overview of only the most important elements of your report. Even a long report may have a short executive summary. The third preliminary is the *statement of originality*, a formal statement by the authors declaring that the report is their own work and that all borrowed material has been appropriately acknowledged.

2   *Introduction*

Like an essay, a report must have an introduction, and this introduction serves a similar purpose. It indicates the purpose of the report; what issue or problem you are going to investigate, its significance and, if appropriate, a hypothesis. Importantly, and unlike an essay, a report's introduction should not indicate the findings or outcome of your report. This information should be saved for later on.

3   *Main sections*

As with essay writing, these sections need to follow a logical sequence; remember, the sequence helps you to communicate your findings and interpretations. You need a section that is normally called a *literature review* (as discussed in Chapter 5). In this section you need to include some discussion of the previous scholarship about the issues you are investigating. By doing this you are gaining credibility in the eyes of your audience; your literature review says to the reader: 'take me seriously because I have done all this research'. Another section to include is one on *methods*. The *methods* or *methodology* section is important because the method that you select will have a great effect on your findings. Therefore, the reader needs to know how you did your research. Finally, after showing that you've read the work of others and have a clear understanding of your methodology, you turn to your *findings*. Here, you will explain what you found or discovered, your solution to a problem, or your judgment about someone else's.

4   *Conclusions and recommendations*

You might also comment on the suitability of the methodology that you employed, and how that methodology affected the outcome of your investigation. In the conclusion you summarize the main points that the report has made. The recommendation section then provides a number of suggestions for action that can solve or ameliorate the problem you have investigated.

Do not forget that liberal use of headings and subheadings, often numbered in some way, will guide your reader through these sections. In fact, developing suitable headings and sub headings will help you plan these sections. Generally, you should have no more than three levels of heading, which you can indicate by changes in typography (font size, bold, italics).

There are times when a lecturer may set a short report (as opposed to an essay) as an assessment task in which case the foregoing detailed and lengthy report format can be shortened considerably; you would not be expected to provide an executive summary. It is not likely to have any original research to report and so will not have a methods section. If in doubt, clarify the style of the report required with your lecturer.

PARAGRAPHS: THEIR ROLE IN ESSAYS AND REPORTS

As well as the macro-structure of an essay or report, there are also expectations about what could be called the micro-structure, and particularly paragraphs. We have discussed the structure and features of a paragraph in the previous chapter and in this chapter we link those points to developing an argument or presenting an explanation or other functions.

Each paragraph makes one major point, or one component of a single broader point. A paragraph can also be organized around a single function, for example, cause-effect, classification or comparison/contrast, and are written accordingly. The length of a paragraph can vary, but in academic writing they usually comprise four to seven (average length) sentences. A paragraph must be long enough to develop its main idea adequately. The quality of your paragraphing will have a huge effect on the overall quality of the essay or report.

Sometimes student writers find themselves with paragraphs that are either too long or too short. If your paragraphs are too long then it may be an indication that more than one topic is covered in that paragraph. Conversely, if paragraphs are too short, then it might indicate one of two things. First, the points that you are making may not be significant enough to warrant a paragraph of their own. Second, the points are significant but because you have done insufficient research you don't know enough to do it justice. If you are writing a report, then you will find that shorter paragraphs are acceptable and may in many cases be preferable.

Paragraph content

- The supporting sentences, or the body of a paragraph, allow you to develop the idea that you have stated in the topic sentence. A common development is to then point out the significance of the paragraph to the overall position being argued.

  ↓

- You then elaborate the idea by explaining its ramifications, making connections with other ideas, contrasting different ideas and drawing inferences.

  ↓

- Next, you support your idea by providing evidence, and interpreting that evidence, showing how it is linked to your point.

  ↓

- You can then add a 'concluding' or wrap sentence as discussed in the previous chapter, keeping in mind your overall argument, and the place of this particular point within it.

TRANSITION SIGNALS

Transition signals in essays or reports serve two purposes. First, they help your writing flow by linking directly one sentence with another. Such links between sentences make things much easier for your reader, and the longer your essays become the more important it is to make such connections. Sentences are linked in sequence, but this is not their only connection; they are also linked in terms of meaning, and the second role of transition signals is to make this meaning clear. Without a transition, will your reader be able to read the meaning that you have intended? What if you mean 'therefore' but the reader thinks 'despite'? In such a case the reader will completely lose the thread of your argument.

There are many transition signals that you can use

To introduce an example

- for example;
- namely;
- for instance (especially if the example is an event).

To add more information

- moreover, additionally, similarly, likewise, in the same way, furthermore.

(Continued)

(Continued)

To indicate a sequence of points

* firstly, secondly, etc.;
* finally;
* another.

To introduce an alternative position

* in contrast; conversely, paradoxically, alternatively, on the other hand, in a different light, seen (in) this way.

USING EVIDENCE

Using evidence, and clearly acknowledging your use, is a phenomenon that separates academic writing from other sorts of writing. Or to be more straightforward: if your essay or report has no evidence, then it is not academic writing. This need to base opinions and actions on research is also something that you find in professional practice.

As vital as it is, evidence does not make the argument for you, however. Rather, the evidence lends veracity to the claims that you are making. No matter how interesting or thoughtful your views are, if you do support them with evidence taken from your research, they won't be convincing. In fact, if you do not have evidence to support your claims, then your essay, however well written and interesting it might be, is much more an assertion than it is an argument. If you want your point of view to be taken seriously (why would you not?), then you need to support your assertions with evidence.

There are three ways to use the ideas of others in your work: paraphrase, summary, and quotation. We've discussed these in the previous chapter and here focus on the potential problems of using quotations in the context of an essay or report.

You really need to have a good reason to take both the words and ideas of a source, which is what you are doing when you directly quote a writer. Often students 'over quote' and this can give a 'second hand feel' to your argument. The essay starts to read like a compilation of others' ideas, rather than your answer to a question. Additionally, it can be uneconomical as quotations can take a long time to make a point. In a short essay, this may become a liability as well as interrupting the flow of your prose.

So when you find yourself about to use a quotation you should ask why you need to borrow another person's words as well as his or her ideas? Could a summary or paraphrase work as well?

Despite these worries, there are times when a quote is indispensable as a form of evidence. These might be three reasons why:

- By using the words of a significant individual or organization you are borrowing their authority to under-write your argument.
- The quote is really well written.
- The quote goes to the heart of what you are trying to argue.

You might also use a chart, table, or graph from a source in which case you might see using these sources as a form of quotation if you reproduce the whole thing. Alternatively, if you take data from a table or chart then you treat it like you would a summary or paraphrase.

In any case you always need to reference your borrowing: referencing is not limited to direct quotation.

REFERENCING AND PLAGIARISM

In every essay you don't get marks if you don't get your bibliography correct. (SW student)

Referencing is a method for acknowledging the sources from which you have drawn. Referencing has two parts. The first part is called the citation or note; the second is referred to as the list of references or bibliography. The citation or note is a marker in the body of your assignment that indicates where you have used other people's ideas. The list of references or a bibliography is a comprehensive list of all work 'cited' in the assignment that normally appears at the end of the piece of work. This is a very general outline so it is advised that you follow the specific method that is recommended by your university.

Failure to reference correctly is one of the major causes of plagiarism. Plagiarism is a form of academic dishonesty whereby a student claims the work of others as their own in order to pass an assignment. Plagiarism is often the product of weak academic skills, so in improving your written work you greatly reduce the chance that you might plagiarise other people's hard work.

EDITING AND PROOF-READING

These two activities, editing and proof-reading, are often used interchangeably. However, they rightly refer to two different activities. Ideally, you should leave some time between finishing writing your essay or report and attempting to edit it. You'll be surprised by how many more errors you'll discover if you have a break from writing your assignment before trying to edit and proof-read it.

This break might also be a good opportunity to let some else read your assignment. If you have been working intensely on a particular assignment, then you might feel that you have lost your perspective; you may not be able to take a step back from your work to adequately appraise it. This is the moment when a fresh pair of eyes, not wearied by weeks of researching and writing, may be able to see weaknesses that you cannot.

EDITING

Many students submit essays and reports that are really of first draft quality. This is normally a sign that the student has run out of time to truly finish the assignment. Editing can make a palpable difference to your final grade so it is worth spending as much time on this stage in the writing process as possible. Generally, you edit first for structure and then for style (as discussed in the previous chapter).

It is important to edit in the right order. So, if time is pressing, edit for the most important things first. For example, make certain that the essay actually answers the question or performs the correct task. It is wonderful to have beautiful flowing prose but not at the expense of good structure, although there is no reason why you cannot have both if you leave yourself enough editing time.

A good technique that will help you to edit for structure is called 'reverse planning'. To do this take your draft and extract all the topic sentences and assemble them as a list; make certain that this list is in the same sequence as the draft. Read through your list and make certain that the points (topic sentences) are in a logical order; if one or more of the points seem out of place, then it might indicate that the paragraph it was taken from is in the wrong position. This 'reverse planning' is particularly useful when you are producing long essays as it allows you to 'see' the whole text. Obviously, this technique is reliant on the accuracy of your topic sentence. Therefore, what might seem from the list to be a misplaced paragraph might actually indicate an inaccurate topic sentence. So, by 'reverse planning' you are actually editing two structural components at the same time.

Some important questions that you should ask to while editing your assignment:

- Does the essay answer the question/address the task?
- Is there a clear distinction between the introduction, body, and conclusion?
- Are the paragraphs presented in an appropriate sequence?
- Does each paragraph have an adequate topic sentence?
- Does the essay have sufficient evidence?
- Have I referenced properly?
- Have I reached and remained within the word limit?

PROOF-READING

You will edit your essay each time you re-draft it. Proof-reading, on the other hand, is the final step before submitting your assignment. Editing is still concerned with structure and content, but when proof-reading your concern is with language and presentation. Recognizing this is different because there is no point proof–reading your essay or report if you have not finished editing it, otherwise you'll spend time making grammatical or spelling corrections that might later be edited out altogether.

Take a lesson from professional proof-readers. Don't proof-read from the computer screen. Print out your essay and mark your corrections by hand. You might also look at previous assignments, especially those from the same course or lecturer, to check for recurring errors through your written work. You might also find that reading your essay or report aloud to yourself helps you 'hear' problems in the writing that you can't see.

Questions to ask while proof-reading

- Have I removed all clichés?
- Have I avoided using discriminatory language?
- Have I written in the first person? Is this acceptable for this assignment?
- Have I punctuated correctly?
- Spelling?
- Have I written the essay using complete grammatical sentences?
- Does my referencing meet the requirements of my discipline?
- Check punctuation and grammar, and for overuse of similar expressions or words.
- Is there correct and consistent spacing?
- Have I provided a title page and a cover sheet (if appropriate)?

CONCLUSION

The large amount of information in this chapter might seem, at first, to add to your worries about writing. However, the only way to get better at writing is to write and certainly developing your writing is not something that can be achieved in the short term, although there are a few things you can do (like referencing properly) that will have an instant effect. One tactic is to concentrate on improving a particular aspect of your writing, especially one that appears to be a recurrent weakness; if you are consistently told that your paragraphing is weak, then that might be the place to start. You might also like to practise your writing outside the requirements of assignments. For example, after taking notes you might write a 300 word summary of that reading, or you could do something similar with a lecture. Such tasks have added value because they'll also help you come to grips with the course content as well as improving your writing. So you might make slow progress but don't be put off, because part of being a writer of any sort is living with a feeling that you could have done things better, and it is this feeling that helps you improve next time.

Finding out more

Web links

The academic writing resources on the university websites listed at the end of the previous chapter (Chapter 7) are relevant and include sections on essay and report writing.

Books

Similarly, the academic writing guides listed at the end of Chapter 7 include chapters on essay and report writing.
Additional, more specific books are listed below:

Emerson, L. (ed.) (2005) *Writing Guidelines for Social Science Students*, 2nd edn. Southbank, Victoria: Thomson/Dunsmore Press.
Specifically targeted for social science students, this book includes the main genres of academic social science writing.

Peck, J. and Coyle, M. (2005) *The Student's Guide to Writing: Spelling, Punctuation and Grammar*, 2nd edn. Basingstoke: Palgrave Macmillan.
Focuses on spelling, punctuation, and grammar in the context of academic writing. Also includes chapters on essay writing, and writing style.

Redman, P. et al. (2006) *Good Essay Writing: A Social Sciences Guide*, 3rd edn. London: SAGE.
This is a detailed guide to writing essays in the social sciences.

9 ACADEMIC WRITING FOR SOCIAL WORK: GETTING THE STYLE RIGHT

This chapter focuses on specific academic writing tasks relevant to a social work degree programme. It will help address:

- different social work academic writing tasks, including reflective journals, reflections on practice, case study papers, demonstrating competence, portfolios, process records, observation reports and critical incident analysis;
- challenges in knowing how to present unorthodox arguments, issues relating to the talking about self in academic papers, and questions about getting the style right.

In social work, you need so many different writing skills like reports and essays and presentations and policy analysis. (SW student)

If you are taking courses across different disciplines (e.g. psychology, politics, and the humanities) you will be aware that there are different expectations for how to present written material, such as essays. In social work, too, there are unique aspects to student writing. Depending on the nature of the written piece, you may be variously, presenting an academic argument supported by evidence, demonstrating your competence in an area of practice, reflecting on yourself and your values, or analysing an aspect of practice you were involved in. And, in some cases, you might be doing all of these things in the one paper! As discussed later in this chapter, there are some particular challenges for students in writing for social work, not least how to balance academic arguments with more personal reflections.

GROWING TO LOVE WRITING IN SOCIAL WORK

Few would disagree that the hallmark of a good social worker is being a good communicator. We might expect them to be good at forming relationships, have finely honed negotiation skills, and be able to manage a meeting of rowdy practitioners (or students or academics). We might not necessarily expect them to be good writers. But, in fact, an ability to write clearly, purposefully, and for the intended audience is one of the most important of a social worker's skills.

A love of writing emerges for many people in their early school years. Remember when you were asked to write a story or a poem about anything you liked? Unfortunately for many of us, the pressures of writing under exam conditions, adjusting to the rigours of academic convention, and writing up practice-based documents (such as forms, reports, and case records) seem to have taken the joy and creativity out of the writing process.

Once you graduate, you will have the opportunity to write for a wide range of purposes, including making information easily available to service users and communities. You may, in the future also be in a position to write for newsletters, professional, or academic journals, and for conference presentations. So your academic writing tasks are only the beginning of your writing career in social work. We hope that you will experience something of the learning and creativity that can emerge from them and that you will be able to build upon in your later practice.

SOCIAL WORK ACADEMIC WRITING TASKS

The previous chapter looked at essays and reports, which are not specific to but are common in social work education. The focus now is on those tasks that are social work specific. In many cases these tasks relate to practice learning, both on campus and off campus in field placements. A feature of practice learning is writing to facilitate reflection.

REFLECTIVE JOURNALS

Reflective journals can help stimulate awareness of learning experiences and the lessons that can be drawn from them. According to Harris (2008: 315) they 'depict journeys of developing awareness'. For example, in some campus-based courses, you may be asked to keep a reflective journal to document your learning across a term or semester. Journals may also be used to support learning while on a field placement. The extent to which a reflective journal is assessed may vary. Some journals may be treated as a largely personal exercise and may be awarded an ungraded pass as long as certain basic criteria (e.g. length of entries) are met. Other journals may be graded and lecturers may have expectations that they will present both personal reflections and evidence of engagement with academic literature. Sometimes you may be encouraged to provide creative responses to your experiences in a reflective journal. This could include a poem or drawing (e.g. the image you have of your first experience of your field placement agency).

PRACTICE REFLECTIONS

You will probably be asked at some stage in your degree programme to write a paper that reflects on and analyses a piece of practice you were involved in. This might involve a piece of work with an individual client, such as the provision of a case management service. Alternatively it might involve a community or group work intervention, such as work with a lobby group of parents of children with mental health needs. It might also relate to a piece of organizational practice, such as a consultation process leading to the development of an agency's strategic plan. The work may have been short-term or carried out over many months. Or the practice reflection might focus on one specific aspect of the work, such as the phase where relationships were formed. These kinds of papers would be most common in or alongside a field placement.

The purpose of a practice reflections paper may be to stimulate reflective learning, which, as discussed in Chapter 4, is underpinned by a body of knowledge that values experience-based learning. Two other dimensions are worth mentioning. One involves reflections during the process of engaging in action – can you remember what ideas or values were influencing how you behaved at the time? The other involves reflections looking forward to engaging in future action. How would you do things differently next time? Each of these approaches to reflection can help demonstrate learning from experience.

CASE STUDIES

Case study papers, a form of practice reflection, involve focusing on and analysing one specific piece of work (the case). The case may relate to work with an individual client, group, community, or organization. While the requirements for a case study paper would vary a lot between different universities, they might include the following, especially if the focus is on enhancing students' understanding of the common phases of helping relationships:

- Describe a piece of work that has been important for your professional development.
- Explain how you came to be involved in the work and what your role was.
- Outline the context in which the work was carried out (e.g. agency setting) and the structural factors (e.g. available resources) impacting on the work.
- Explore the different stages of your involvement in the work in relation to processes of relationship formation, assessment, intervention or action, and evaluation.
- Identify the knowledge (e.g. research and theoretical knowledge) that you drew upon to inform the work and what knowledge can be used to analyse the practice.
- Highlight the professional skills that were evident in the work, including the use of self as vehicle for social work practice.
- Critique the ways in which power was apparent in the situation, in the context of the work and in your relationship with the client(s).
- Reflect on the personal and professional values evident in the practice and any ethical issues or dilemmas that needed to be addressed.
- Identify the learning gained from the work, areas of strength, and areas for further development.

Case study papers are a common form of writing on practice placements. One third year student commented that carrying out a case study:

… was really good and I learnt a lot through the theory behind what I was doing.

DEMONSTRATING COMPETENCE

As we discussed in Chapter 4, demonstrating practice competence is a common part of the social work student experience. For example, in the UK students and practitioners may be required to demonstrate students' practice competence in line with the key roles of the National Occupational Standards (as discussed in Chapter 1). Universities and field placement agencies set up a number of writing tasks to enable you to demonstrate practice competence, such as a case study assignment. Most commonly it involves completion of a report or standardized form whereby the student and/or their practice teacher explains how the student has met the various standards or practice outcomes. This is an especially important process for students as it requires careful explanation of how the competence was achieved, evidence and examples that illustrate this and, ideally, reflection on the learning that was gained and the areas for further development. The comments provided will need to be specific. For example, compare the following two extracts from social work students' placement reports in response to the social work key role: manage and be accountable with supervision and support for your own social work practice within your organization.

Response 1: While on placement I received regular supervision and participated in team meetings. When I came across difficulties I always consulted with my supervisor and took advice from other team members. I listened carefully to my supervisor's suggestions and tried to put these into practice. Sometimes we role played different responses to difficult practice situations. I was always very aware of the importance of being accountable to my supervisor for my practice.

Response 2: During my weekly meetings with my supervisor we evaluated each of the cases I was involved in and discussed progress so far and any difficulties experienced. For example, in week 6 I was able to talk with my supervisor about my difficulties establishing appropriate professional boundaries with a client, Ms D, who had regularly asked if I would have lunch with her. My supervisor and I discussed some of the literature on professional boundaries and possible responses in these situations. We role played some of these within supervision to see which felt more appropriate. I was then able to follow through with the preferred strategy, which resulted in Ms D acknowledging that the focus of our relationship was to assist her with her difficulties rather than a friendship. From this I learned to be accountable for my practice by openly discussing with my supervisor any practice difficulties and by working with my supervisor to develop and implement alternative strategies. While I was able to clarify my relationship with Ms D, I am aware that I felt very uncomfortable doing this and that I need to gain more experience in talking openly with clients about the nature of our relationship.

While the first response has the benefit of being fairly brief, it is limited through its frequent generalizations (e.g. 'I always consulted') and lack of specific details or examples that provide evidence of competence. The second response explains more clearly how accountability for practice was maintained (e.g. through case evaluations during supervision and engaging with the literature) and gave a specific example where this improved the quality of the work (i.e. enabled appropriate professional boundaries to be established). The student then goes on to highlight what learning was gained and where they needed more experience. The recognition that more learning is needed in no way undermines the demonstration of competence in this area; rather it highlights the student's self-awareness and commitment to accountability in practice.

PORTFOLIOS

Those who have worked in the creative industries (such as graphic design and advertising) would be familiar with the concept of a portfolio as a collection of material designed to demonstrate and showcase a person's achievements and learning. In social work education, portfolios are being used to assist in the demonstration of practice competence and to provide a document that can be used in job applications (Fitch et al., 2008). However, they might also have more formative purposes: by being asked to bring together and present examples of your practice, your capacity to reflect on this practice is enhanced. Thus, 'students would be reflecting on the development of all their professional skills in the process of creating their emergent professional identity' (Fitch et al., 2008: 38). You could include in your portfolio examples of different forms of practice writing (such as psycho-social assessments and organizational analysis), statements evidencing competence and learning, and feedback from supervisors, colleagues, and service users. A recent initiative has been electronic portfolios (ePortfolios) which make it easier over time to collate and present a wide range of material (Fitch et al., 2008).

OBSERVATION REPORTS AND NARRATIVES

Observation is one of a repertoire of skills that you need to develop to apply in your future work. For example, you will need to be aware and make sense of the contexts in which you engage with people, as well as the behavioural indicators of how people are feeling. In addition, you will need to make particular observations, such as when assessing parenting skills or when evaluating the quality of care provided in a residential setting. And you need to be able to do this in a way that is respectful of people's circumstances, rather than in a way that is perceived as being overly judgemental. If you have had the experience of having your practice observed by a supervisor or tutor, you are probably aware of the power of the observer and how uncomfortable it feels to be closely scrutinized. Social work educators are increasingly recognizing the value of observation-based learning, including the writing up of this learning through reports and narratives.

There are a couple of ways of carrying out observation for social work. Structured observation, which may involve a checklist of things to look for, involves a scientific and objective approach to observation. In writing up a report of a structured observation, you might present data about the frequency of certain observed behaviours.

For example, in an observation of a young child you might record the demonstration of attachment behaviours. Unstructured observation, which is more in synch with a reflective learning approach, involves also attending to the experiences of the observer. Here it is recognized that what you observe is partly constructed by your own way of viewing the world, such as your values and how you are feeling on a particular day. In addition to reporting what has been observed, the writing up of this kind of observation would involve a subjective account of the experience of doing the observation. So, in the previous example, you might choose to write about how your own experience as a parent and your current worries about your own children shape the way you view a child's attachment behaviours. The book by Le Riche and Tanner (1998) provides a valuable overview of issues in observation for social work.

PROCESS RECORDING

Another reflective learning technique is process recording. Like a case study assignment, process recording focuses on one piece of work; in particular on one specific interaction related to this work. Most commonly this is an interview (or part of an interview) between a practitioner and a client. However, it would be confined to this. Process recording can be carried out on other types of one-to-one communication (such as between a practitioner and their supervisor) and on group interaction (such as family therapy sessions or inter-agency meetings).

What is process recording?

It is a way of recording an interview between a worker/student and a client and usually involves:

1   an outline of the purpose of the interview, the nature of prior contacts, and function of the agency;
2   a detailed description of the interaction, including verbal and non-verbal communication, often recorded verbatim;
3   analysis of the content of the interaction, which might include an analysis of how the phases of helping relationships – such as bio-psycho-social assessment, relationship building and treatment – were evident in the interaction;
4   a reflection on the worker/student's role in the interaction, what they were trying to achieve and an assessment of their effectiveness. (Walsh, 2002)

You can structure a process recording into columns so that reflections may be made alongside the detailed account. As almost everyone who has carried out a process recording will say, one of the biggest challenges is recalling what took place in the interaction. But if anxiety about this can be overcome, it is surprising how much can be remembered. According to Neuman and Friedman (1997) process recording is an invaluable tool to assist students in their conscious use of self in practice and in their application of theory in practice. This, they say, is achieved through the '3 Rs' of process recording: recall, writing, and reflection.

CRITICAL INCIDENT ANALYSIS

Critical incident analysis examines a particular experience or situation in order to draw out learning. Here the focus is on specific incidents that were important for you – this may be because you found them particularly challenging or because they extended your learning. The incidents do not have to have to be dramatic, just significant for you. These accounts may be structured (e.g. by recording on a form) or be unstructured in a narrative format.

Fook (2002) suggests reflecting on and analysing the following in a critical incident report:

- patterns and themes apparent within the narrative;
- who the potential players are in the situation and your relationship to them;
- whose perspectives are apparent and whose perspectives are missing;
- what interpretations were made and what influenced these interpretations;
- what might have been some different interpretations of the situation;
- what assumptions are apparent in the narrative and how these relate to things like theories, values, and political systems;
- who (or what systems) benefits and who loses from these assumptions;
- where the gaps or biases are in the narrative; and
- how your understanding of power emerges from the experience. (Fook, 2002)

According to Lam et al. (2007) students' narratives on critical incidents on field placements reveal challenging emotions, but they see these as the starting points for critical reflection, including increased self awareness. Rather than seeking to avoid risk, direct exposure to risk and uncertainty (within bounds) provides unique learning for students.

EXAMS

Most social work students will have to write under exam conditions. The exam could be:

- closed book: no material apart from stationery is allowed into the exam room;
- open book: certain materials such as text books and notes are allowed;
- take home: an open book exam that is completed at home over a specified time frame (e.g. three days).

The types of questions presented in these exams could range from multiple choice and short answer questions through to lengthy essays. Questions might aim to ensure you have acquired particular knowledge and these might be prepared for by rote learning (memorizing). Other questions might involve you critically analysing a particular case example or piece of legislation or policy. Or you might be asked to apply learning across different parts of your study. For example, if you have studied case management you might be required to evaluate the positives and negatives of a particular approach to case management in working with young offenders. For these kinds of questions you will need to go beyond rote learning, and prepare by gaining a very good understanding of the material and by thinking about how it can be critiqued. See the box below for some tips for closed book and open book exams. Relevant to all types of exams is the importance of carefully reading the question and breaking down what is being asked. For essay style questions, the principles discussed in Chapter 8 are just as relevant in exams as they are in handed-in assignments: prepare an introduction, body, and conclusion; think about your paragraph construction; and write as legibly as possible. You should make clear with your lecturer or tutor beforehand whether or not referencing is required and the extent to which references should be provided (especially for closed book exams).

Tips for closed book exams

- Take time to read the exam paper thoroughly.
- Before writing an essay, jot down all ideas and prepare them into an essay plan.
- Make sure you clearly identify which question you are answering especially if there are multiple essays.
- Make sure you allocate time to each question according to the marks awarded.
- Try to answer the question in the first sentence of an essay.
- If you run out of time, answer in point form.

Tips for open book exams

- Don't underestimate the time needed to prepare for them – you won't have time to learn the material while you are completing the exam.
- Don't just copy large amounts of material from the text book – this will be treated as plagiarism.
- Organize your material carefully so that you can retrieve it quickly – e.g. have contents pages or indexes of books close to hand, use post-it notes to mark key places, and prepare lists of key information.
- If you are doing a take home exam make sure you have the time available and have a quiet space to complete it.
- For essays, don't use too many quotations – your own analysis is what is important.

CHALLENGES IN SOCIAL WORK ACADEMIC WRITING

NEGOTIATING 'POLITICAL CORRECTNESS'

Debates about 'political correctness' are common in social work education. This rather derogatory term emerged in the 1980s as a conservative strategy for denigrating progressive concerns for equality and anti-discriminatory practices, especially with respect to the use of racist and sexist language. While social work values reflect what might commonly be seen as progressive ideas – such as the promotion of social justice – there is no doubt that social work, as a profession, attracts people with a wide range of political views, including conservative perspectives. And even those who ascribe to progressive ideas sometimes speak out against dogmatic ways of thinking about or implementing social work's ideals.

What has this got to do with writing social work papers? Well, a concern sometimes expressed by social work students is that their lecturers and tutors expect them to 'toe the party line' and not to challenge prevailing thinking. While it is important not to discount that this might be happening, it is possible that it is the way the unorthodox views have been argued and evidenced that may be the cause of concern for academic staff, rather than the content of the arguments. Questions to consider when presenting unorthodox arguments include the following Are you aware of and have you acknowledged the prevailing wisdom in the field? Do you understand it and can you point to its limitations? What is the evidence (e.g. research-based evidence) for an alternative view? One student noted:

> Students might feel that they have to write to suit the left wing or a right wing. … It should be just purely you understanding and grasping the content of the subject and then writing for what is needed for the criteria sheet. (SW student)

Having said this, it is important to recognize that some social work academic papers require a demonstrated commitment to social work values. If this is built into the marking criteria for a paper, then it stands to reason that arguments that run counter to this (e.g. ones that actually do reflect discriminatory attitudes such as sexist or homophobic views) will be negatively evaluated. Nonetheless, from a critical reflective position, it is important to scrutinize prevailing ideas and discourses and the ways in which power is variously expressed. Anti-oppressive practice, which in the UK was subject to a debate about 'political correctness' (see McLaughlin, 2005), involves challenging power inequalities including those generated through professional intervention. This requires a high level of self-awareness and a capacity to critically evaluate your own impact on other people. This reflexivity is a far cry from a rigid and dogmatic articulating of progressive values as put forward by those who critique 'political correctness'.

TALKING ABOUT SELF

A feature of some social work academic writing is the requirement to balance academic arguments with reflection on your self and your practice.

> I think most reflection is personal. So we had to look at a piece of academic work that we had been learning on practice [placement] and then dissect it and reflect on our practice and what we had learnt. (SW student)

One of the challenges involved in writing about yourself is working out what is appropriate to talk about in relation to the paper at hand. What aspects of your personal experiences and/or identities are relevant to the academic argument or to the practice that is being evaluated? In most cases, the paper will not be an invitation to divulge a wide range of personal information. So, in a paper that critiques an assessment interview you carried out with a male client who is about the same age as your father, it may be appropriate to reflect on how the client reminded you of your father (if this was the case) and what the impact of that might have been on how you communicated with the client. However, in maintaining the focus of the paper on the assessment interview, it may not be appropriate to go into substantial detail about the nature of your relationship with your father and your attempts to reconcile conflicts that occurred in your teenage years.

A Student Dilemma

Consider the situation of a student who has been a refugee. The kind of introspection required in reflective papers is likely to be confronting and may raise issues of mental health and wellbeing. This may mean that the student may need support and assistance – it is important to acknowledge this. This student will also be faced with deciding how much to disclose of their personal background. They might be quite happy to disclose that they have been a refugee, but they may not be happy to disclose that they have a learning disability. In a university context in which you may be required to conceal your identity when submitting assignments, this student will have to be particularly careful whether or not they reveal having been a refugee given that they may be the only person in that class in this situation and thus would be identifiable.

A dilemma for all students is the tension between being honest, on the one hand, and presenting yourself as only competent and capable, on the other. While social work academics and practice teachers will be looking to see evidence of your competence, this includes competence in self-reflection and ongoing personal and professional learning. So a reasonable level of honesty is important. Acknowledging mistakes and demonstrating how one would do things differently next time are the hallmarks of ethical and reflective practice. Students who are able to reflect on these matters are in a much better position than those who feel they need to always present themselves as being 'in control'.

GETTING THE STYLE RIGHT

I didn't know what she meant by reflective work, but the lecturer gave us some great examples and that made it clear. (SW student)

We have just discussed the wide range of writing social work students are required to produce. An aspect of all writing is knowing your audience. Different audiences require variations in the grammatical person and type of voice used in different papers. For example, if the paper involves primarily academic-based argument, it may be appropriate to write it in the third person singular and in the passive voice (e.g. 'in this paper it is argued that …'). This is a common convention at universities. However, if the paper involves substantial personal or practice reflection, then it may be more appropriate to write it in an active voice and in the first person singular (e.g. 'in this paper I argue that …') or, if it were a group project, the first person plural (e.g. 'in this paper we argue that …'). As discussed in previous chapters, different universities may also have their own convention about what is appropriate. Or, if unsure if the first person is allowed, it would be worth checking with your lecturer.

> *You are taught not to speak in the first person, so any time you are writing in the first person sometimes I find that a bit awkward. Like, how do I transfer from the academic writing to the first person? And still make it sound academic? (SW student)*

When you do write in the first person, such as in reflective writing, you must pay close attention to using evidence for the conclusions that you reach. For example, you may not be able to reject conclusively a point well established in the research literature on the basis of your own experience, but you may be able to say that your experience may warrant further attention in future studies.

CONCLUSION

Social work academic writing is challenging in part because it serves dual purposes. First, it is often directed towards students' demonstrating understanding and competence. This is usually what is the focus of assessment. Second, it is used as a means of facilitating learning and, as we have seen in this chapter, often a particular type of learning – reflective learning. However, as we have suggested, while it may be tempting and understandable to present oneself and one's practice well, you may gain more (and lecturers may appreciate it more) when you are able to be upfront and honest about the challenges you have faced.

Finding out more

Websites

The Scottish Social Services Council provides a useful overview of critical incident analysis. In addition, the links on the left hand side of the site provide access to a wide range of material on reflective/reflexive writing.
http://cactusid.heehawdevelopment.com/LO2-HowToDoIt-Frameworks-CriticalIncidentAnalysis.html

The University of North Carolina has a good selection of resources to inform social work writing.
http://ssw.unc.edu/students/writing

(Continued)

Most universities will have resources for you to access to help you prepare for exams. For example the University of Greenwich has some useful resources that can be downloaded.
http://www.gre.ac.uk/studyskills/exams

Books

Burns, T. and Sinfield, S. (2008*) Essential Study Skills: The Complete Guide to Success at University*, 2nd edn. London: SAGE.

Le Riche, P. and Tanner, K. (eds) (1998) *Observation and Its Application to Social Work: Rather like Breathing*. London: Jessica Kingsley.

10 DISCUSSIONS, PRESENTATIONS, DEBATES AND ROLE PLAYS: UP CLOSE AND PERSONAL

In this chapter we discuss the types of spoken communication on which, as a social work student, you will be assessed and in which you will be expected to become skilful. This will assist you to:

- facilitate discussions;
- prepare and structure a presentation;
- use visual aids effectively;
- participate in debates;
- participate in and benefit from role plays.

As a social worker in the making, you need to be able to communicate clearly and effectively face-to-face with your student peers, your lecturers and tutors, your future clients and colleagues. Social workers rely on personal communication for most of their professional practice, so rehearsing the variety of spoken and non-verbal communication forms you need is an important part of social work education. You will not be surprised to hear that being a skilled verbal communicator is a professional social work requirement and is evident throughout the Social Work Codes of Ethics already discussed in earlier chapters. It is always an essential criterion in social work positions that usually require 'excellent oral communication' or 'excellent face-to-face counselling skills' or just 'excellent communication skills'. Good oral communication, in whatever form, is recognized everywhere as one of the essential social work skills.

Most of us think we don't need to practise speaking. After all we've done it since we can remember; it is as natural and easy as breathing.

Well, it is not quite so simple. There are many different contexts and types of spoken communication you will engage in as a student and in the future as a practising social worker and all require skills you may not have developed in your everyday life. You will make formal individual and group presentations, give verbal reports, lead discussions in seminars, participate in role plays and conduct debates. And you need to match verbal skills with listening skills. Attentive listening is an integral part of verbal communication, especially in social work practice (Baldry et al., 2005). If you don't listen actively, you won't be able to give a genuine response and you won't be respecting the person who has just spoken.

You may not have intended to become a teacher but most social workers, at some time in their career, are community educators. Learning to engage a variety of people and get across information and ideas verbally is part of a social worker's repertoire and so is included in your university study.

Remember, while you're a student is the time to practise these skills with others in your class and with your teachers, all of whom want you to succeed and will give you invaluable feedback, support, and encouragement. Critical and constructive comments on your verbal communication are like gold – consider them carefully and use them to hone your skills. When the roles are reversed and you are the person giving peer feedback, give the kind of feedback you know, from your own experience, will strengthen and enhance the other person's ability to communicate. This works both ways – your classmate benefits and so do you because you learn a little more every time you pay critical attention to someone else's presentation.

Now we shall look at some detailed discussion of the types of spoken communication on which you will be assessed and in which you will be expected to become skilful.

DISCUSSIONS

We all join in discussions about the everyday or matters of import over a meal, walking together to the bus or train, or after seeing a good film or hearing a startling news item. Discussions in a group tutorial though are more formal, structured and purposeful. You are expected to demonstrate that you can engage in these sorts of discussions and are sometimes assessed on participation in class on this basis. Discussions are important aspects of studying because they help you to explore and understand the topic at hand more deeply; they improve your ability to think critically because you have to listen to, follow and respond to arguments and ideas in the flow of conversation and you get the chance to hear other students' views often on controversial matters such as birth control, sentencing of offenders and involuntary hospitalisation. Discussions assist you to develop confidence in speaking publicly in groups, improve your listening skills and spoken expression and they may even challenge you to change your attitude on a particular matter.

If you find participating in discussions hard and anxiety producing try attending as many seminars and tutorials as possible and observe how other students participate, ask questions, support or disagree with arguments and make critical comments. Practise joining in these more formal discussions at every opportunity. Ask your tutor for some feedback about your discussion skills.

At some point in your social work degree you will probably be required to lead a discussion.

Eight steps in leading a discussion

1. Introduce yourself and group members.
2. State the discussion topic.
3. Help manage equal participation time.
4. Listen carefully to all contributions.
5. Invite quiet members to participate.
6. Field comments and questions in a fair and enabling manner.
7. Summarize points.
8. Thank the group for the discussion. (adapted from Wallace, 1980; Hollet et al, 1989)

PRESENTATIONS

'That didn't work, let's do it again', until eventually you just feel so much more confident; you're doing things that are real. (SW student)

Giving an oral presentation, whether solo or with a group, to your peers and lecturers can be a rather daunting prospect, especially the first time. Be assured, everyone feels nervous about standing up and speaking in front of an audience – even your lecturers. It's akin to being an actor, and like an actor, you will improve and become less nervous with practice. But unlike most actors, social workers' presentations are usually interactive, adding the dimension of listening and responding, to the dimension of communicating information and ideas, so in this respect it is like (good) teaching.

Seminar formats are those in which you may give a short paper or speak to a PowerPoint presentation on a set reading or research topic to a group of your peers, and then facilitate discussion on the points you have raised.

Giving a seminar or tutorial presentation usually involves:

- reading background material;
- preparing the presentation;
- leading the discussion;
- preparing handouts;
- preparing thought provoking questions;
- submitting a written assignment based on the presentation.

PREPARING

Giving an effective presentation is like painting an old house – it depends largely on good preparation.

Make sure you understand what it is you're being asked to do: do you have to present an argument or explain or discuss something; are you being expected to be critical? Have clear objectives before you start and if you're unsure ask your tutor or lecturer.

Research your topic: you will have to demonstrate in your talk an understanding of the main points of the article, chapter or the topic of the presentation. This may necessitate going further afield and reading related articles, books, reports or documents. Express your own ideas and opinions regarding the topic and show that you can evaluate the strengths and weaknesses in the material you are dealing with.

Time limit: presentations have time limits and you are likely to lose marks as well as your audience's interest if you ramble on. Check how long you have; work out how much material you can fit into the time allotted; divide your material into sections with headings and have these in front of your audience on a screen or a handout; delete less important points rather than racing through the talk; if you are using a written 'script' allow around 400 words for each five minutes.

If you are making your presentation available in some written form make sure it is accessible to persons with disabilities. This may mean making it available before hand to the university equity and diversity or disability unit for translation to audio or Braille or some other appropriate format.

STRUCTURING

A presentation is no different from a written assignment or paper in that it should be well structured. It needs an introduction, a body and a conclusion (see McEvedy et al., 1986 for a more detailed discussion of a flexible use of this pattern). Poorly structured talks will confuse and frustrate.

INTRODUCTION

Capture your audience's attention at the beginning. You might first introduce yourself then start with a question. 'Why are so many people still homeless in this country? Today I'm going to throw some light on this from the reading …' or 'What are some of the best ways to work with people who have mental illness? This morning I'm going to highlight the key practice approaches discussed in …'. You might then tell your audience what you will cover with a brief outline of the main points. Make sure important terms are defined.

Where appropriate use a visual to grab attention 'In front of you is a chart showing the rise in child abuse notifications over the past ten years.'

BODY

This is where you develop your main points and present examples and evidence. Use an organizing principle such as a chronological, order of importance or thematic approach. For example, if the topic is the development of community work you might take a chronological approach but if it is a discussion of the meaning and importance of social justice then you might take a thematic approach.

To emphasize a key concept, you can repeat it. For example, 'Listening is a crucial social work skill: listening responsively; listening attentively; listening actively …'. You could have it as a single word or phrase on the screen whilst you discuss it.

Flagging that a point or idea is now going to be dealt with or will be coming up later in the talk is an effective way of keeping people's attention: 'I'll be commenting on Foucault's analysis of control shortly …'; or 'Having presented the benefits of risk management I'll now move on to criticisms of its use.'

CONCLUSION

Don't introduce any new material in your conclusion. Use it to bring together the main ideas and information you have covered. Use a transitioning phrase like 'In conclusion …' to let your audience know that's where you are now heading; restate the main points; and demonstrate that you have done what you set out to do.

ON WITH THE PRESENTATION

Now you are well prepared. You know your topic, have your prompt cards or your PowerPoint or whatever aids you might be using set up, and it is presentation time.

Even when you are a seasoned social worker presenting a report to a ministerial committee you will benefit from taking a couple of quiet minutes before you have to face the audience. Find a quiet corner, take a few deep breaths, concentrate on the here and now, and you will feel more grounded and ready to present. If you feel nervous, tell your classmates, they will understand and it's one way to break the ice.

SPEAKING WELL

This is where one of the benefits of rehearsing shows up. If you have rehearsed in front of friends or at least taped yourself, you will have picked up how you sound when you are presenting. You can begin to develop vocal variety. Vary the volume, pitch and rate of your speech. If you don't vary your speech, you will send everyone to sleep no matter how interesting the content. Pace should be varied, for example slower and measured for a serious point needing emphasis and faster to lend excitement and urgency. If you tend to use fillers like Uhmms and Aaahs a lot, having a well-prepared script can help overcome that. But you can also be deliberative in changing such a habit by being aware of how you present and deliberately not using such distracting fillers.

ENGAGING YOUR AUDIENCE

Whether the audience is your class peers or the Director of the Social Services Department, a presentation has to be engaging, otherwise it will not achieve its goals of informing, convincing and challenging.

Use examples and illustrations that will resonate with your audience. Your student peers will connect with something familiar at university or currently in the media or that has been discussed in lectures. Talk directly to your audience, make eye contact, and invite participation. Look at them. Comment on reactions such as 'I can see some of you look bit puzzled – let me explain further ...' and invite them into the presentation with phrases such as 'I wonder what you think when you see these poverty figures ...' and give space for people to respond. Don't let such participation opportunities take over though, otherwise you won't get your presentation finished. You can use phrases such 'Thank you for those comments ... I now want to move on to ...'

Leave time for questions and discussion at the end of the presentation so your audience can:

- clarify misunderstandings;
- ask for further information;
- raise other issues;
- disagree and present an alternative view.

Handling discussion time

- Listen carefully to the whole question or comments.
- Stay relaxed and focus on the point at hand.
- Summarise the question or comment to be sure you have understood it.
- Address the whole audience when answering.
- If you don't know the answer say so.
- Respond to the topic, not the tone of the question or comment (especially if it is negative).
- When finished ask whether that has addressed the point. (adapted from Mohan et al., 1997)

VISUAL AIDS

Visuals are effective in engaging your audience and illustrating points – but the old adage 'a picture is worth a thousand words' is only partly true. Any visuals you use should support and add to your points and ideas not take over.

Using PowerPoint as a presentation tool is common. You certainly don't have to use it but if you do there are some general principles to consider:

- Messages on each slide should be clear and concise.
- Use colour imaginatively.
- Use large font that can be seen easily from the back of the room.
- Don't:
  - Ignore the audience.
  - Turn off all the lights.
  - Just read aloud what is written on the slides.
  - Put a lot of text in each slide.
  - Use too many slides.
  - Over-use animation.

Photos, DVD and other visual clips are good as long as you don't overuse them and they are directly relevant to the topic. Social work students use brief clips from YouTube, movies, TV series and documentaries, as well as song lyrics to illustrate social issues and practice to great effect.

Presentation Preparation Checklist

- Do I know what I'm doing?
- What's my audience like?
- Do I have a brief summary of my presentation?
- Have I prepared the presentation?
- Have I rehearsed the presentation?

First: ask yourself

- What is my reason for giving the talk?
- What topic am I speaking about?
- To whom am I speaking?
- What are my goals:
  - to inform
  - to explain
  - to entertain
  - to persuade
  - to share
  - to stimulate/inspire?
- What do I want my audience to do, think and feel when I am finished?

Second: do an audience analysis

- Age?
- Size?
- What do they already know about the topic?
- What are their attitudes and feelings towards the topic?
- What are their attitudes and feelings towards me?

Third: write a single summary of your talk

- Choose the main points you will use to develop this summary.
- Decide the order in which they will be presented.
- Decide on a means of supporting each point: visuals, examples, stories.

Fourth: prepare

- The introduction: be clear and engaging.
- The body: work out how you are going to move from one point to another.

(Continued)

(Continued)

- The conclusion: how are you going to finish the talk?
- Prompt cards or notes.
- Visual aids/equipment.

Fifth: rehearse

- In front of an audience (could be friends, family or your study group) including all the props you intend to use.
- The time it takes including leaving time for questions and discussion.
- By recording your presentation to evaluate how it sounds – most of us are unaware of how we speak. Finding out that you use 'Uhmm' between every sentence or that you talk too fast, for example, means that you can work at correcting such habits.

GROUP PRESENTATIONS

A group presentation, in which a number of students work on a reading or research topic and present their findings to the rest of the class, is another common learning and teaching approach in social work education. Many social work positions are embedded in a team so throughout your career you will need to pull together team presentations for various purposes, for example to convince senior managers of the benefits of an approach your team is taking or to peers working in the same area.

All the suggestions made in the previous section on presentations apply to group presentations with one large difference. You have to prepare with the group; that is be thoroughly organised and agreed on who is presenting what, and on the timing – you will not be a popular group member if you take up most of the time and leave your co-presenters with only a few minutes to give their part of the presentation. Group presentations are often more difficult than solo ones because all group members need to be well attuned to each other. Everyone has to pull their weight in the preparation (often a site of group conflict) and all need to be clear on the main messages and key information being given. This means rehearsals are especially important – you are a member of an ensemble, perhaps not quite Broadway, but nevertheless you are giving an ensemble performance.

DEBATES

People confronting me ... has helped me to establish what my personal beliefs are. (SW student)

Debates provide opportunities for the development of the key social work graduate attributes of values clarification, critical thinking and analysis, research, synthesis of information, oral communication skills and team work/cooperation (Kennedy, 2009). You bring all these attributes together in a debate to try to persuade listeners that your position on an issue is valid. This is a particularly demanding task when you are on the opposite side to your personal values position. You may have participated in debates before, so debates at university should be seen as a chance to improve your critical argumentation skills and to understand and stretch yourself further. Social work programmes are urged to include debates as both learning and assessment tools, especially in social policy courses, precisely because they develop and test these critical thinking core graduate attributes (Gregory and Holloway, 2005).

CONDUCTING A DEBATE

Formal debates usually consist of three participants on each side arguing for or against the proposition. You may be assigned the affirmative side arguing: 'The poor are responsible for their poverty'. You and your team, no matter what your personal views may be, must assemble all the arguments for this proposition. In doing so you gain an understanding of why many people in society, agencies, and government might hold this position and, as a social worker in the making, you gain clarity regarding your own views and values, and why people hold differing views on such contentious social matters.

You and your team would divide the roles with the first speaker opening with the broad arguments, along with evidence supporting the proposition. In this case these might be points such as each person makes their own future and fortune and it is a matter of an individual's determination, hard and honest work. Your second speaker might elaborate with details such as those who are poor do not try to better themselves. They are lazy and expect society to support them via the welfare state that develops dependency and they are more likely to engage in crime instead of participating in civil society. Your final speaker will rebut the opposition's arguments that are likely to be around structural inequality, lack of opportunity, class, sex, and race discrimination.

Just as with group presentations, debate preparation requires the development of strong cooperative teamwork and a clear focus on the issues. If you are being assessed on your performance in a debate, your lecturer will be looking for evidence of good research skills, clear critical thinking, good teamwork and capacity to think 'on your feet'.

ROLE PLAYS

The role play was awesome. It makes me feel like it is actually real now, I will be a social worker in two years' time; this is really cool. (SW student)

Role plays may be used in social work education at all levels as a learning device for students in acquiring the knowledge, values, and skills of social work practice (Hargreaves and Hadlow, 1997: 61). The key element of role plays is that they create an 'as if' setting; that is they ask participants to act as if they were in the position of the person they are playing and to practise doing the things required in that particular role. They assist you to develop empathy with people with whom you work as you put yourself in their shoes; build your confidence as you role play being a social worker; and sharpen your listening and responding skills as you must listen carefully to understand what is happening in the interaction and respond appropriately in an unrehearsed setting.

> Playing out roles can then be a vital educational tool to introduce new or enhance existing skills in the learner's practice repertoire; to focus upon an alternate or more profound comprehension of practice situations or life events; to create pertinent personal affect experience, thereby sensitizing learners' and others' affect processes and feeling states as well as the learners' capabilities for identification. (Maier, 2002, online)

> … role playing is used for its promise to engage learner and instructor alike in a specific learning experience. It can be employed for its rich transfer of learning potential to each participant's own learning repertoire. (Crawley and Gerrand, 1981, cited in Maier, 2002, online)

Role plays are used not only for student learning but also in therapy and in assessing clients' capabilities (see for example Yardley-Matwiejczuk, 1997) so they are tools you may well use in your future practice. Ogilvie and Douglas (2007) point out that role plays are becoming established in the virtual realm as learning and teaching tools, so you may find yourself engaging in a role play via the internet in both learning and assessment modes.

Below is an example of a role play at the University of Wisconsin helping social work students to experience what it feels like to be a social work client. It enabled students to draw on anti-oppressive practice, to develop empathy with clients, and to consider the impact of policies and systemic procedures on persons having to navigate social care systems.

Role-play puts social work students in shoes of poor

Nearly 75 students enrolled in UW-Green Bay's undergraduate program in Social Work took part in a poverty-simulation exercise that dramatized the daily frustrations experienced by individuals and families.

The purpose was to stimulate student thinking and awareness about the challenges people with limited resources may encounter as they try to improve their lives and to enhance social work course content to reflect current economic conditions and rising poverty.

Students played the role of family members and individuals who needed help with balancing limited monthly resources and navigating community resources. Students, in their various assigned roles, were given scenarios which required them to go from table to table to apply for services, make loan payments, obtain childcare, find transportation and maintain basic living standards for their families.

Students remarked that they quickly became frustrated with the system's red tape, lengthy waits for services, and a sense of being discriminated against by virtue of being poor. Results of the exercise are addressed in class as students consider their future work as social workers.

http://blog.uwgb.edu/inside/index.php/log-news/news/03/12/social-work-poverty-simulation/

The student quoted at the beginning of this section on role plays was reflecting on the benefit of role playing a social worker. This is both a common teaching and assessment method. It is educational because you act as if you were a social worker in a hospital, or child protection, or community agency and have to draw on the lecture, tutorial, and reading material you have had so far to help you think through what you would do in this circumstance in a safe and developmental situation. You are usually asked to reflect critically on what you did in the role play and your peers and teacher do the same and discuss with you good and not so good approaches and strategies you used.

Debates and role plays are especially effective in pushing you into reflexivity, one of the practices you will be challenged by whilst a student and a lifelong habit all social workers need to develop (D'Cruz et al., 2007; Arnd-Caddigan and Pozzuto, 2008).

CONCLUSION

Social work is a profession vitally dependent upon all forms of communication. In this chapter how to study, develop skills in and prepare for assessment in spoken and face-to-face communication has been explored. The importance of preparing for and practising different forms of verbal communication including listening is emphasized throughout social work programmes with the aim of equipping social workers in the making with these essential skills in professional life.

Finding out more

Web

The University of Surrey has a good step by step guide to oral presentations:
http://www.surrey.ac.uk/Skills/pack/pres.html

Speaking and listening is well covered in the Monash University's learning support pages:
http://www.monash.edu.au/lls/llonline/speaking/index.xml

Manoram and Pollock discuss the benefit of role plays in teaching and learning and give clear and useful outlines of approaches to running debates in class:
Manoram, K. and Pollock, Z. (2006) *Role Play as a Teaching Method*. Meekong Learning Initiative accessed at http://www.usyd.edu.au/mekong/

The Designing Flexible Learning Framework site provides examples of on-line debates on social issues:
http://designing.flexiblelearning.net.au/gallery/activities/debates.htm

REFERENCES

Abrahamson, E. and Freedman, D.H. (2007) *A Perfect Mess: The Hidden Benefits of Disorder*. New York: Little, Brown and Company.

Adams, R. (2002) 'Developing critical practice in social work', in R. Adams, L. Dominelli and M. Payne (eds), *Critical Practice in Social Work*. Palgrave: Basingstoke.

Anyon, Y. (2008) Review of the book 'Meeting the Needs of Students and Families from Poverty: A Handbook for School and Mental Health Professionals', [electronic version], *International Journal of Social Welfare*, 17: 410–11.

Arnd-Caddigan, M. and Pozzuto, R. (2008) 'Use of self in relational clinical social work', *Clinical Social Work Journal*, 36: 235–43.

Australian Association of Social Workers (AASW) (2002) *Code of Ethics*, 2nd edn. http://www.aasw.asn.au/about/ethics.htm#Ethics%20Framework

Australian Association of Social Workers (2003) *Practice Standards for Social Workers: Achieving Outcomes*. Barton: AASW.

Baldry, E., Bratel, J., Dunsire, M., and Durrant, M. (2005) 'Keeping children with a disability safely in their families', *Practice: Social Work in Action*, 17 (3): 143–56.

Beresford, P. and Evans, C. (1999) 'Research and empowerment', *British Journal of Social Work*, 29: 671–7.

Boud, D. and Knights, S. (1996) 'Course design for reflective practice', in N. Gould and I. Taylor (eds), *Reflective Learning for Social Work*. Aldershot: Arena.

Bovens, M. (1998) *The Quest for Responsibility*. Cambridge: Cambridge University Press.

Bradley, G. (1992) 'Stress and time management workshops for qualifying social workers', *Social Work Education*, 11 (1): 5–15.

Bradshaw, J. and Finch, N. (2003) 'Overlaps in dimensions of poverty', *Journal of Social Policy*, 32 (4): 513–25.

Branfield, F., Beresford, P. and Levin, E. (2007) *Common Aims: A Strategy to Support Service User Involvement in Social Work Education*. London: Social Care Institute for Excellence.

Briggs, S. (1999) 'Links between infant observation and reflective social work practice', *Journal of Social Work Practice*, 13 (2): 148–56.

British Association of Social Workers (BASW) (2002) *Code of Ethics*. http://www.basw.co.uk/Default.aspx?tabid=64

Bryman, A. (2004) *Social Research Methods*, 2nd edn. Oxford: Oxford University Press.

Clanchy, J. and Ballard, B. (1991) *Essay Writing for Students: A Practical Guide*. Sydney: Longman.

Cohen, M.B. and Garrett, K.J. (1999) 'Breaking the rules: a group work perspective on focus group research', *British Journal of Social Work*, 29: 359–72.

Craswell, G. (2005) *Writing for Academic Success: A Postgraduate Guide*. London: SAGE.

Crawley, J. and Gerrand, J. (1981) 'The use of role play in fieldwork teaching', *Contemporary Social Work Education*, 4 (1): 55–64.

Davies, M. (ed.) (2000) *The Blackwell Encyclopaedia of Social Work*. Oxford: Wiley-Blackwell.

D'Cruz, H., Gillingham, P., and Melendez, S. (2007) 'Reflexivity, its meanings and relevance for social work: a critical review of the literature', *British Journal of Social Work*, 37: 73–90.

Drury Hudson, J. (1997) 'A model of professional knowledge for social work practice', *Australian Social Work*, 50 (3): 35–44.

Dunleavy, P. (2003) *Authoring a PhD: How to Plan, Draft, Write, and Finish a Doctoral Thesis or Dissertation*. Basingstoke: Palgrave Macmillan.

Field, D., Gilchrist, G. and Gray, N. (1989) *First Year University: A Survival Guide*. Ontario: Ontario Institute for Studies in Education.

Fitch, D., Peet, M., Reed, B.G. and Tolman, R. (2008) 'The use of e-portfolios in evaluating the curriculum and student learning', *Journal of Social Work Education*, 44 (3): 37–54.

Fook, J. (2002) *Social Work: Critical Theory and Practice*. London: SAGE.

Gibbs, A. and Strirling, B. (2010) 'Reflections on designing and teaching a social work research course for distance and on-campus students', *Social Work Education*, 29 (4): 441–9.

Gilgun, J.F. (2005) 'The four cornerstones of evidence-based practice in social work' [electronic version], *Research on Social Work Practice*, 15: 52–61.

Giltrow, J. (2005) *Academic Writing: An Introduction*. Peterborough, Ontario: Broadview Press.

Glaser, B.G. and Strauss, A.L. (1967) *The Discovery of Grounded Theory: Strategies for Qualitative Research*. New York: Aldine Publishing Company.

Grant, B.M., Giddings, L.S. and Beale, J.E. (2005) 'Vulnerable bodies: competing discourses of intimate body care', *Journal of Nursing Education*, 44 (11): 498–504.

Gregory, M. and Holloway, M. (2005) 'The debate as a pedagogic tool in social policy for social work students', *Social Work Education*, 24 (6): 617–37.

Gross, R. (1999) *Peak Learning*. New York: Jeremy P Tarcher/Putnam.

Hargreaves, R. and Hadlow, J. (1997) 'Role-play in social work education: process and framework for a constructive and focused approach', *Social Work Education*, 16 (3): 61–73.

Harris, M. (2008) 'Scaffolding reflective journal writing – negotiating power, play and position', *Nurse Education Today*, 28: 314–26.

Hawking, S. (1988) *A Brief History of Time*. London: Bantam Press.

Healy, K. (2005) *Social Work Theories in Context: Creating Frameworks for Practice*. Basingstoke Palgrave Macmillan.

Healy, K. and Mulholland, J. (2007) *Writing Skills for Social Workers*. Los Angeles: SAGE.

Hollett, V., Carter, R., Lyon, L. and Tinios, E. (1989) *In at the Deep End*. Oxford: Oxford University Press.

Honey, P. and Mumford, A. (1986) *The Manual of Learning Styles*. Maidenhead: Ardingly House.

Hughes, M. and Heycox, K. (2010) *Older People, Ageing and Social Work: Knowledge for Practice*. Sydney: Allen and Unwin.

International Federation of Social Workers (IFSW) (2004) *Ethics in Social Work: Statement of Principles* http://www.ifsw.org/en/p38000324.html

Kamler, B. and Thomson, P. (2006) *Helping Doctoral Students Write: Pedagogies For Supervision*. London: Routledge.

Kennedy, R.R. (2009) 'The power of in class debates', *Active Learning in Higher Education*, 10 (3): 225–36.

Kolb, D.A. (1984) *Experiential Learning: Experience as the Source of Learning and Development*. New Jersey: Prentice Hall.

Lam, C.M., Wong, H. and Leung, T.T.F. (2007) 'An unfinished reflexive journey: social work students' reflection on their placement experiences', *British Journal of Social Work*, 37: 91–105.

Le Riche, P. and Tanner, K. (eds) (1998) *Observation and Its Application to Social Work: Rather Like Breathing*. London: Jessica Kingsley.

Learning Centre (UNSW) (2009) *Academic Writing Skills for Undergraduate Social Work Students*. Kensington, NSW: The Learning Centre, University of New South Wales. accessed at: http://www.lc.unsw.edu.au/

Maier, H. (2002) 'Role playing' accessed at: http://www.cyc-net.org/cyc-online/cycol-0102-roleplay.html

Marsh, P. and Fisher, M. (2005) *Developing the Evidence Base for Social Work and Social Care Practice. Using Knowledge in Social Care Report 10*. Bristol: SCIE.

McEvedy, M., Packham, G. and Smith, P. (1986) *Speaking in Academic Settings: Oral Skills for Seminars, Discussions and Interacting with Supervisors*. Melbourne: Nelson.

McLaughlin, K. (2005) 'From ridicule to institutionalization: anti-oppression, the state and social work', *Critical Social Policy*, 25 (3): 283–305.

Mohan, T., McGregor, H., Saunders, S. and Archee, R. (1997) *Communicating: Theory and Practice*, 4th edn. Sydney: Harcourt Brace.

National Association of Social Workers (NASW) (1996) *Code of ethics* http://www.socialworkers.org/pubs/Code/code.asp

Neuman, K.M. and Friedman, B.D. (1997) 'Process recordings: fine-tuning an old instrument', *Journal of Social Work Education*, 33 (2): 237–43.

O'Connor, L., Cecil, B. and Boudioni, M. (2009) 'Preparing for practice: an evaluation of an undergraduate social work "preparation for practice" module', *Social Work Education*, 28 (4): 436–54.

O'Hagan, K. (2007) 'Competence: an enduring concept?', in K. O'Hagan (ed.), *Competence in Social Work Practice: A Practical Guide for Students and Professionals,* 2nd edn. London: Jessica Kingsley.

Ogilvie, A. and Douglas, K. (2007) 'Online role plays and the virtual placement: aiding reflection in work integrated learning, Ascilite Conference', accessed online at: http://www.ascilite.org.au/conferences/singapore07/procs/ogilvie.pdf

Peters, P. (1985) *Strategies for Student Writers*. Milton (QLD): Wiley.

Pollard, K.C., Miers, M.E. and Gilchrist, M. (2004) 'Collaborative learning for collaborative working? Initial findings from a longitudinal study of health and social care students', *Health and Social Care in the Community* 12 (4): 346–58.

Pugh, R. (2009) Review of the book 'Challenging Welfare Issues in the Global Countryside', [electronic version], *International Journal of Social Welfare*, 18: 323–4.

Rudestam, K.E. and Newton, R.R. (1992) *Surviving Your Dissertation: A Comprehensive Guide to Content and Process*. Newbury Park, CA: SAGE.

Saunders, P. (2003) 'Stability and change in community perceptions of poverty: evidence from Australia', *Journal of Poverty*, 7 (4): 1–20.

Saunders, P., Naidoo, Y. and Griffiths, M. (2008) 'Towards new indicators of disadvantage: deprivation and social exclusion in Australia', *Australian Journal of Social Issues*, 43 (2): 175–94.

Saleebey, D. (ed) (2008) *The Strengths Perspective in Social Work Practice*, 5th edn. Boston: Allyn and Bacon.

Schön, D.A. (1983) *The Reflective Practitioner*. London: Temple Smith.

Spafford, M., Schryer, C.F., Campbell, S.L. and Lingard, L. (2007) 'Towards embracing clinical uncertainty: lessons from social work, optometry and medicine', *Journal of Social Work*, 7 (2): 155–78.

Strauss, A. and Corbin, J. (1998) *Basics of Qualitative Research: Techniques and Procedures for Developing Grounded Theory*, 2nd edn. Thousand Oaks, CA: SAGE.

Sturhahn Stratton, J., Mielke A., Kirshenbaum, S., Goodrich, A. and McRae, C. (2006) 'Finding a balanced life: factors that contribute to life satisfaction in graduate students', *Journal of College & Character*, 7 (8): 1–10.

Swales, J. and Feak, C. (2004) *Academic Writing for Graduate Students: Essential Tasks and Skills*, 2nd edn. Ann Arbor: MI University of Michigan Press.

Taylor, I. (1996) 'Facilitating reflective learning', in N. Gould and I. Taylor (eds), *Reflective Learning for Social Work*. Aldershot: Arena.

The Learning Centre UNSW (2009) *Academic Skills for Bachelor of Social Work Undergraduate Program*. Kensington, NSW: The Learning Centre, University of New South Wales.

Tipper, B. (2006) Review of the book 'Childhood Poverty and Social Exclusion: From A Child's Perspective', [electronic version], *International Journal of Social Welfare*, 15: 363–5.

Topss (2002) *The National Occupational Standards for Social Work*. Leeds: Topss.

Turney, D. (1997) 'Hearing voices, talking difference: a dialogic approach to anti-oppressive practice', *Journal of Social Work Practice*, 11 (2): 115–25.

Wallace, M. (1980) *Study Skills in English*. Cambridge: Cambridge University Press.

Wallace, M. and Wray, A. (2006) *Critical Reading and Writing for Postgraduates*. London: SAGE.

Walsh, T.C. (2002) 'Structured process recording: a comprehensive model that incorporates the strengths perspective', *Social Work Education*, 21 (1): 23–34.

Webb, S.A. (2001) 'Some considerations on the validity of evidence-based practice in social work', [electronic version], *British Journal of Social Work*, 31: 57–9.

White, S. (2009) 'Fabled uncertainty in social work: a coda to Spafford et al.', *Journal of Social Work*, 9 (2): 222–35.

Witkin, S.L. and Harrison, W.D. (2001) 'Editorial: whose evidence and for what purpose?', [electronic version], *Social Work*, 46: 293–6.

Worsley, A., Stanley, N., O'Hare, P., Keeler, A., Cooper, L. and Hollowell, C. (2009) 'Great expectations: the growing divide between students and social work educators', *Social Work Education*, 28 (8): 828–40.

Yardley-Matwiejczuk, K.M. (1997) *Role Play: Theory and Practice*. London: SAGE.

Zerubavel, E. (1999) *The Clockwork Muse*. Cambridge, MA: Harvard University Press.

INDEX